Conversations with Albert Murray

Literary Conversations Series

Peggy Whitman Prenshaw
General Editor

Conversations
with Albert Murray

Edited by
Roberta S. Maguire

University Press of Mississippi
Jackson

Books by Albert Murray

The Omni-Americans: New Perspectives on Black Experience and American Culture. New York: Outerbridge & Dienstfrey, 1970. (Republished 1989 as *The Omni-Americans: Some Alternatives to the Folklore of White Supremacy* in New York by Da Capo Press, Inc.)

South to a Very Old Place. New York: McGraw-Hill, 1971. (Republished 1991 in New York by Vintage Books. [Random House] and 1995 by Modern Library [Random House].)

The Hero and the Blues. Columbia: University of Missouri Press, 1973. (Republished 1995 in New York by Vintage Books.)

Train Whistle Guitar. New York: McGraw-Hill, 1974. (Republished 1989 in Boston by Northeastern University Press.)

Stomping the Blues. New York: McGraw-Hill, 1976. (Republished 1989 in New York by Da Capo Press, Inc.)

Good Morning Blues: The Autobiography of Count Basie (as told to Albert Murray). New York: Random House, 1985. (Republished 1995 in New York by Da Capo Press, Inc.)

The Spyglass Tree. New York: Pantheon Books, 1991. (Republished 1992 in New York by Vintage Books.)

The Seven League Boots: A Novel. New York: Pantheon Books, 1996.

The Blue Devils of Nada: A Contemporary American Approach to Aesthetic Statement. New York: Pantheon Books, 1996.

Copyright © 1997 by University Press of Mississippi
All rights reserved
Manufactured in the United States of America

00   99   98   97   4   3   2   1

The paper in this book meets the guidelines for permanence and durability of the Committee on Production Guidelines for Book Longevity of the Council on Library Resources.

Library of Congress Cataloging-in-Publication Data

Murray, Albert.
    Conversations with Albert Murray / edited by Roberta S. Maguire.
        p.   cm. — (Literary conversations series)
    Includes index.
    ISBN 1-57806-007-9 (cloth : alk. paper). — ISBN 1-57806-008-7 (paper : alk. paper)
        1. Murray, Albert—Interviews.   2. Afro-American authors—20th century—Interviews.   3. Afro-American intellectuals—Southern States—Interviews.   4. Afro-American aesthetics.   I. Maguire, Roberta S.   II. Title.   III. Series.
PS3563.U764Z464   1997
813'.54—dc21   97-2626
                                                   CIP

British Library Cataloging-in-Publication data available

Contents

Introduction

Albert Murray is fond of talking about what marks some artists as great: They blaze trails well in advance of other artists, finding ways to "stylize particulars," as Murray would say, so that their compositions—whether in painting, literature, or music—move beyond the representational to capture something ineffable, something akin to the human spirit. Paul Cezanne is one such artist for Murray, as are Ernest Hemingway and Louis Armstrong. Each paved the way for later greats, like Pablo Picasso and Georges Braque, like John Coltrane; even William Faulkner had to learn from Hemingway, according to Murray.

What Murray does not say is that he, too, occupies a place in that pantheon of trailblazers. And yet he clearly belongs there, for it is Albert Murray who perceived that the underpinnings of an African American cultural aesthetic, which he would argue is the quintessential American aesthetic, are the blues and jazz—the blues and jazz as ritualized expression. It is this last component of ritual that is peculiarly Murrayan, and so distinguishes him from his good friend and fellow writer Ralph Ellison, who also saw the potential for translating the structure of the blues and jazz into literary art. Without Murray's pioneering work in such books as *The Omni-Americans* (1970), *The Hero and the Blues* (1973), and *Stomping the Blues* (1976), all of which argue for seeing the blues and jazz not only as the foundation of an aesthetic but as an indicator of African American and, hence, American identity, it is difficult to imagine Houston Baker's seminal *Blues, Ideology, and Afro-American Literature* (1984), or Cornel West's *Race Matters* (1993).

But Albert Murray remains an enigma for much of America's reading public; on one hand identified by Duke Ellington as "the unsquarest person I know" and introduced as "the dean of African American letters" at a gathering celebrating the publication of *The Norton Anthology of African American Literature*, Murray is just as likely to be called one of the American literary scene's "best-kept secrets" (Salisbury, 1993). He remains a secret because he cannot be categorized. As soon as you think you've got him fixed, he writes a new book of fiction or essays, gives another interview that moves him squarely out of the box he's just been put in. Is Murray, then, inconsistent? Contradictory? Yes—and no. If he's inconsistent, it's because he's human and, as such, is a product of what he perceives as the natural state of life: chaos. But he is absolutely consistent in what he does with that chaos: He stylizes it.

And that stylization, evident in each of his books, is every bit as evident in his interviews. This book brings together twenty interviews with Murray conducted over the last twenty-plus years, beginning with an interview that took place shortly after his second book, *South to a Very Old Place,* was published, and ending with a previously unpublished interview with the editor conducted during the summer of 1996. Each selection reveals a man who clearly enjoys the interview situation, who has a story to tell and is anxious to tell it and have it be understood. For, as Murray himself suggests in his interviews, it is narrative—storytelling—that makes the human condition bearable.

But the story Murray tells is usually not one filled with the facts of his own personal history, beyond those that he deems relevant for his development as "an all-purpose literary intellectual." He is quick to divulge the literary artists who have been most important to him: Thomas Mann, Hemingway, James Joyce, Faulkner, T. S. Eliot, among others. And he is equally quick to explain that he found the writers of the Harlem Renaissance "indispensable," yet ultimately "too provincial" and so "inadequate for [his] purposes" ("To Hear Another Language," 1978). Of course, he also talks about how the work of such geniuses of jazz as Louis Armstrong and Duke Ellington have contributed to his development as a literary intellectual, and how cultural critics such as Constance Rourke and John Kouwenhoven, likely viewed as slightly off-beat by the academy today, helped him see how he could meld the ideas of his literary and musical forbears through "extension, elaboration, and refinement." By way of these explanations, Albert Murray reveals himself to be the very composite that his books argue Americans are.

That composite emerges gradually through the pieces compiled here. While the topics covered are remarkably consistent—for example, he speaks of his disdain for sociological "stereotyping" of cultures and individuals in almost every interview—he nearly always offers a new take on them, challenging any narrow assumptions we might make about the import of his ideas. And he even comes to reveal some personal history that he forcefully argues is largely irrelevant for any understanding of him and his work (the "emotional truth" of it, he maintains, is sufficient and is contained in his novels). But the details of his own beginnings and subsequent experiences growing up in post-World War I Alabama help provide a fuller context for his thought than that which was previously available. His quiet, personal revelations in the final interview underscore why and how his conception of the composite American is so thoroughgoing. The value of this collection is that, taken together, the interviews grant scholars and general readers a broad view of a man whose influence on American art has been—and continues to be—profound.

The interviews contained herein have been arranged chronologically, beginning with a relatively short piece by Hollie West that appeared in the March 26, 1972, edition of the *Washington Post* and culminating in several lengthy conversations with Murray from 1996. Fully half of the interviews in the book were conducted in the 1990s, which surely suggests that as Murray has published more books, we have taken more notice of him; but it may also suggest that he was initially ahead of his time, since the ideas contained in his early work are the same ones he is working with today. Walker Percy intimated this latter possibility when he sent his friend Murray a copy of his review of *The Omni-Americans,* written over a year after the book's initial publication: "Too bad your thesis is not fashionable, Al, but you will probably be canonized posthumously if it is any consolation" (WP to AM, December 12, 1971).

From the first, interviewers have also recognized that Murray was going against the grain, even if they found it hard to articulate just what he *was* doing. Hollie West, for example, ends his piece by emphasizing Murray as black protest writer, using his own words for support: "Still," Murray is quoted as saying, "one of the things that horrifies me is that some white guy is always explaining black people to me." Although secondary to the focus on social science, other important—and often controversial—Murrayan themes emerge in this interview, including the idea that African American culture derives from a response to slavery, incorporating "resilience, strength and the blues spirit," rather than from a memory of Africa.

Fred Beauford's piece in the summer 1972 issue of *Black Creation* probes more deeply Murray's thinking about black identity while investigating Murray's contention that the white southerner has a greater ability to get at the essence of the black experience than the white northerner—even though Murray agrees with Beauford that white southerners have been largely responsible for fostering negative images of blacks. But these images, Murray argues, become less detrimental for African Americans in the face of those put forth by white northerners who, he argues, are steeped in the abstract arguments of social science. Murray says, "the traditional stereotypes of the South [are] so ridiculous that you could, just by existing, counterstate the image," whereas northern social science abstractions that emphasize the repression and oppression of African Americans, having caught the fancy of black intellectuals, were far more insidious.

If these early interviews focused on Murray as a spokesman for black identity—a role he denied he wanted or should have (Gelfand, 1974)—they also hinted at what has emerged as his primary preoccupation: delineating the function of art, of aesthetics, as a means to struggle against the chaos of existence that confronts every man and woman alive. With Fred Beauford, although he did not linger on the topic, he was most direct: "[A]rt . . . is about . . . man's struggle for sanity against chaos." He returns to this point two years later in his 1974 interview with Marvin Gelfand, and does riffs on it in any number of interviews, including Beverly Grunwald's in 1976, Beverly Bateman's in 1978, Louis Edwards's in 1994, and Tony Scherman's in 1996. One might expect a man who perceives chaos at the heart of human existence to be dour, gloomy. Not Murray: He may have the blues, but he embodies the principle of blues music, which is a celebration of humankind's ability to put the blues off for another day. As evidence of that, one need only note how so many interviewers describe Murray's raucous laughter and animated demeanor.

So how does Murray see himself? As an all-American writer, which he made clear recently at a PEN/Faulkner reading in Washington, D.C. But, as the conversations in this book also make clear, he is an American writer by way of his regional and cultural identity, both of which retain tremendous importance for him. Back in 1974, he was urging scholars to think of him in terms of being a southern novelist (Gelfand), as part of a tradition that includes Mark Twain, Faulkner, Robert Penn Warren. The idea emerges again in the transcript of a television program aired in Nashville in 1992, and again in the 1996 interview with the editor of this volume. But in the last interview, he qualifies his identification with other southern writers: While they are an "intimate part of [his] heritage," they are "aesthetic" as opposed to "ideological" relatives. In his mind, he is and he isn't a southern writer.

Similarly, Murray is and is not a black writer—or Negro writer, in his preferred terminology. At once linking himself to the "Afro-U.S. tradition of idiomatic storytelling," which, he says, "is largely concerned with the exploits of epic heroes who are involved with the complexities of human motives and with the contradictions of human nature and with the ultimate inscrutability of nature as such," he also distances himself from "U.S. Negro writers" whose stories, he claims, "seldom rise above the level of one-dimensional patently partisan social case histories" (Berry, 1977). In a fascinating 1978 conversation with friends Romare Bearden, Alvin Ailey, and James Baldwin reprinted in this volume, Murray sums up his approach to race and racial politics: "You don't have to go out with a flag about blackness." And neither need one go out with a flag about victimization, Murray insists in a 1991 interview with Gene Seymour; he argues it is that flag which has stymied contemporary African American writers.

For Murray, victimization does not define African American culture; as he indicated to Jason Berry, heroics do. And he makes clear through a number of interviews, beginning with Gelfand's in 1974 and culminating in Tom Piazza's and Tony Scherman's in 1996, that heroism is the primary, maybe the only, subject worth writing about. If he uses his nonfiction to *tell* us the components of Murrayan heroism—with the ability to improvise, he reminds his interviewers, as the crucial first component—he uses his fiction to *show* us heroes; Scooter, the main character in each of his novels, is his clearest example. Murray is reaching for ideals in his fiction, since he sees them as finally more fundamental, more important than the real (Scherman, 1996). Without a concept of the ideal, he warns us, "civilization could blow up any day" (Piazza, 1996).

In accordance with the format of other volumes in the Literary Conversations series, the previously published interviews offered here appear uncut and unedited, aside from silent corrections of typographical or factual errors and regularized treatment of book titles. Additions have been made to one interview, Tony Scherman's piece for *American Heritage,* at the request of Mr. Murray. Bracketed to distinguish them from what was originally published, the additions represent material initially included as part of the interview. Appearing in print for the first time are the last interview in the volume, which was conducted by the editor, and the transcription of John Seigenthaler's interview for Nashville Public Television, both of which have been edited for publication.

The interviews selected for this volume delineate the range of Murray's thinking and work. Some very good pieces of journalism have been excluded from this volume either because they were too short, relied less on Murray's own words than other pieces covering the same ground, or appeared during a year when there was an abundance of interviews from which to choose. In the last case, interviews were chosen that either presented a topic Murray frequently spoke of in a new way or offered a picture of Murray in a new light. It should be noted that Murray himself does not find that the interviews in the volume always accurately represent his conversation or the context in which comments were made; Joe Wood's interview, for example, he sees as an attempt to distort his points. But even when interviewer and interviewee do not see eye to eye, what is revealed is that Murray's work demands passionate response.

I wish to extend my gratitude to the many interviewers and publishers who have granted me permission to reprint these interviews, to the many scholars and Murrayites who have helped me in my quest to locate those interviewers and publishers, and, above all, to Albert Murray, whose generosity is an ideal to which to aspire.

RSM
January 1997

Chronology

1916	12 (?) May, born in Nokomis, Alabama, to Sudie Graham and John Young; adopted by Hugh and Mattie Murray, who then moved from Nokomis to Magazine Point, Alabama
1935	Voted best all-around student at Mobile County Training School; awarded tuition scholarship to Tuskegee Institute; begins attending Tuskegee in the fall
1939	Receives B.S. degree from Tuskegee
1940	Returns to Tuskegee from graduate school at the University of Michigan to teach literature and composition
1941	Marries Mozelle Menefee, who graduated from Tuskegee in 1943
1942	In New York, re-encounters and begins a lifelong friendship with fellow Tuskegean Ralph Ellison
1943	Enlists in United States Army Air Forces
1946	Meets Duke Ellington; ends World War II active duty and transfers to Air Force Reserve; returns to teach at Tuskegee
1947	Enrolls in graduate program at New York University
1948	Receives M.A. degree from NYU and returns to Tuskegee
1950	Summer, meets Romare Bearden in Paris
1951	Resumes active duty in Air Force
1955	Stationed in Morocco for Air Force duty
1958	Stationed in California for Air Force duty
1961	Closed Air Force facility at Long Beach Municipal Airport and is transferred to Air Systems Command at Bedford Air Force Base in Massachusetts
1962	Retires from Air Force with rank of major; settles in New York City

Conversations with Albert Murray

Waging War on Social Science

Hollie I. West / 1972

From *The Washington Post,* March 26, 1972, p. G3. © 1972, The Washington Post. Reprinted with permission.

NEW YORK—Albert Murray, teacher, novelist, essayist, folklorist and raconteur, is waging his own war against social scientists.

His chief targets are Daniel Moynihan and Kenneth Clark, primarily for the pronouncements they have made about blacks.

Murray, a retired Air Force major and now visiting professor of English at the University of Massachusetts, bristles at mention of Moynihan and the government report the former presidential aide wrote about matriarchal patterns in black families. He calls it "a propaganda vehicle to promote a negative image of Negro life in the United States."

Murray has a similar reaction to the work of Kenneth Clark, whose theories were partly used as the basis for the 1954 Supreme Court school desegregation decision. He says Clark's book *Dark Ghetto,* a study of black life in Harlem, projects a black wretchedness exceeding the stereotypes found "in most of the books written by white racists to justify segregation."

Sitting in the book-lined apartment in Harlem he and his wife Mozelle, a public school teacher, share, Murray explains his invective: "Social scientists are playing one-upmanship with blacks. If you look at a community, tribe or people, you look at all the interrelationships of their lives. If you simply talk about their incomes, where they live or how many children they have, you leave out a lot of the stuff of life.

"There's been an overextended subscription to social science as the answer to what blacks are. Social scientists run surveys to substantiate theories. The older social scientists had the discipline of the humanities. They always thought life was a mystery."

Murray complains that the media has parroted social science theories as truth. "Many white journalists and newspapers' readers presume to explain the Negro in terms of these reports," he says. "It really burns me up—the way whites use the term ghetto, and blacks are following suit. The word has lost all its original meaning. We're not living in ghettoes. We're not forced to live anywhere."

1

Murray, 55, trim and 5-feet-9, made some of these points in his 1970 book, *The Omni-Americans,* and he takes up similar strains in his new book, *South to a Very Old Place.* But the latter book is essentially an account of a trip he took South to discover the region's history and new meaning for blacks and whites. Murray was also going home for he grew up in Mobile, Ala., and was educated at Tuskegee Institute.

Written in odd-metered prose and shifting images, the book takes shape from Murray's "effort to play literary vamps and intellectual riffs equivalent to the musical ones Duke Ellington feeds his orchestra from his piano."

Murray travels north to New Haven to talk with Southern historian C. Vann Woodward and then heads South to interview Robert Penn Warren and journalists Jack Nelson and Joe Cummings. He writes about Atlanta University, a citadel of black education, uses people's voices in Mobile to explain black and white attitudes toward using the words "nigger" and "boy."

Murray examines the sensibility of William Faulkner, Thomas Wolfe, Walker Percy, Hodding Carter and several other writers. He approaches the book with a broad cultural orientation—culture in the anthropological sense.

"If I were studying society," he says, "I'd want to know about its art forms, how the people talk and what kind of crafts they use. This brings us back to social science. A social scientist should have a knowledge of folklore, dance, music, language—the whole cultural complexity.

"I look at the type of rhetoric I'm using—I could call my style the chitterlings of the Waldorf. I can deal with abstractions that have to do with Kenneth Burke's theories or deal with the downhome dimension."

Murray has a disarming capacity for combining the abstract and downhome and relating them in a binding human way. Paintings by Romare Bearden and Norman Lewis hang on his wall. He has hundreds of records from Bessie Smith to Schönberg. His bountiful knowledge of French wines is sometimes expressed in the guttiest street corner talk.

"It doesn't matter if your great-great-great grandfather was a monkey, you can still order something on the menu," he says. "What we should be celebrating is the flexibility of human nature. No one has to go back to Africa to prove his heritage. We survived slavery with a higher degree of humanity than the slaveowners. We came out of it (slavery) with resilience, strength and the blues spirit."

Murray's "pet project" these days is promoting Frederick Douglass, the 19th century black abolitionist, former slave, diplomat and writer, whom he thinks history has forgotten.

Says Murray: "Frederick Douglass is a better illustration of the American story—the American as self-made man—than the founding fathers. Douglass invented freedom for himself. *My Bondage* and the *Narrative of the Life of Frederick Douglass* should be required reading for students.

"If we're going to drop something out of the anthologies, we should drop *Walden Pond.* Thoreau was out there three miles from Emerson and the Alcotts in the most civilized part of the country, and at the same time fugitive slaves were dealing with nature in the most basic ways. Thoreau was playing boy scout games compared to slaves.

"I taught this at Colgate and the white kids accepted it. They were more interested than black kids, I suppose, because the blacks thought they had heard all that."

Murray, who has also taught at Brandeis, Columbia and the New School for Social Research, is working on a novel he hopes to finish this year and a book about the philosophy of literary form.

He says his writing is protest but also other things. "I want to look at life in a cosmic sense—how man has evolved. Still, one of the things that horrifies me is that some white guy is always explaining black people to me."

A Conversation with Al Murray

Fred Beauford / 1972

From *Black Creation,* 3, no. 4 (Summer 1972), pp. 26–27.

Al Murray pulled his chair less than two feet in front of me and leaned his body forward until his face was just inches away from mine. We sat high above the ground in a Black middle class enclave on 132nd Street overlooking parts of Harlem and a grand view of the George Washington Bridge leading into Jersey. Inside the apartment the booklined walls and tasteful furniture make one more than conscious, as Murray himself likes to point out, that Harlem contains more than one world.

As he began to talk about his new book, *South to a Very Old Place,* his eyes took on a definite glow and his trim 55-year-old body took on added youthfulness as our conversation turned into an almost two hour marathon ranging from "social science stereotyping" to Black Nationalism.

The book, whose idea came from an assignment from *Harper's Magazine,* is a series of syncopated free form "riffs" told by an ex-Southerner, retired Air Force major, sometimes college professor and full time writer on the many visions he encountered during his trip back home.

"Willie Morris (then editor of *Harper's*) and I had been talking for several years about certain Southern lifestyles. And I had been talking about that 'seed store feed store court house square' dimension of Southern intellectual life—journalists, writers and so forth—who dealt with actuality rather than abstractions. Especially when they began to address themselves to problems.

"Whereas, many times Northerners, New York liberals especially, tend to deal with abstractions. And along with the abstractions, a lot of sentimentality emerges and out of that comes some easy compassion and condescension. It ends up very negative. And in any case, it paints an inaccurate picture of the Black experience."

Most would agree with Murray that Northern liberals do cloud their vision of Blacks behind foggy screens of graphs and birth/death statistics, but many would then point out to him that it is that home-spun Southerner that he speaks of who is most responsible for most of the images that whites in this country hold about Blacks.

"Over the years, yes," he agreed, "but," he quickly added, "I am very

4

much concerned with pointing out that Northerners today are very much involved with replacing the traditional stereotypes with a new kind—a social-science stereotype. And this, in my opinion, is worse. He's now a pathological stereotype. He's got the trappings of science. They're writing us out of humanity with science.

"Whereas, some of the traditional stereotypes of the South were so ridiculous that you could, just by existing, counterstate the image. For example, if they say that you are happy-go-lucky and you're successful at business you have simply counterstated the argument. There are a number of ways that actuality or reality counterstates those traditional stereotypes. But what we are suffering from now is the full weight of a new piety of scientific terminology that has been built around the Black experience, which is seen in terms of social science, which I call the new folklore of white supremacy."

As far as Murray is concerned a Faulkner, who he says was "steeped in the folklore and wisdom of Uncle Remus and Aunt Hagar," could give his Black characters a "greater humanity," while most Northern intellectuals look to Europe, and more specifically, to Marx and Freud, and thereby miss the essential essence of the Black experience in this country.

"For example," he pointed out, "one of the things that gets left out of the Marx/Freud formulations is that they miss the centrality of the church in American life among Blacks; that the dynamics that operate in political action are essentially church dynamics. So that it is not so unusual that Powell, King or Malcolm X were ministers. And that certain reprimands that go with the church go with the political rhetoric. So that berating sinners and making exaggerated statements like "if you don't bring your child to church you don't love God . . .' "

You mean, translated politically, that if you don't vote for me you don't love Black people, don't you?

"Yes. Yes," he answered, "it gets to that."

It is also deeply implied in the book that there is almost an alliance between some of the new Black writers and the Marx/Freud intellectuals.

"Yes," Murray answered, "that is implied and I think that many of the new writers have been led to that particular orientation, not so much by intrinsic drives and things in themselves and coming out of their experience as human beings. To a certain extent they have accepted the formulations about themselves that other people have imposed on the experience. They are playing the other man's game rather than looking into the experience that he has lived, that his father has lived, that his grandfather and great grandfather have lived.

"And that's what I keep talking about when I talk about the social-science approach. It does not give the writer a broad enough experience to deal with. We are more than oppression and repression. Where you have a rich literary output coming out of the experiences of a people you have a richer self image and a more useful and a more functional self image no matter what happens. We can't afford to be reduced to oppression and repression. Just two types, is that all we are? I know that to say that is political but we can't confuse politics with the deeper implications of our experience. So far we have left that up to the musicians, but the writers must deal with it as well."

Murray's point was well taken indeed. But still, given the facts, the people who say that, in fact, the overriding reality for Blacks in this country *is* oppression and repression and that anything that the artist does that does not deal with these everyday facts of life is, at best, frivolous, is also a well taken point. I asked Murray what he felt.

"Well," he answered, "that is a man who is into political action. But I am simply saying that fine, you have politics, but politics have to come out of something richer than one dimensional or two dimensional formulas of what human life is about. I mean anytime a man says that art and all these things are frivolous, then what kind of society is he trying to create? What will they do after they are all well fed?"

What about those who say that all art is political?

"All art has political implications, but all art isn't political propaganda but mainly propaganda for humanity. It is about man's fate; man's struggle for sanity against chaos. If an artist must give everything to a certain person's program that reduces him to writing slogans or painting signs, then he is not doing his job in the community which is to give it a richer image of itself to give a base for formulating answers which will be richer and more meaningful."

What about the significance of other people's cultures and literature; should our leaders also read as much of that as possible?

"They got to," he answered, now waving his hands in forceful movements, "anything that is relevant to mankind. This is another technology. This is a technology of ideas. Anything that anybody has done anywhere that is going to help you understand human motives is valuable. That is why we study other languages so that ideas that have had the greatest impact in the world are available to us. And it has nothing to do with the glorification of a certain culture or a certain group of people, but rather to put us in contact with anything that man has discovered that will enhance another man's life."

As we ended the interview Murray felt sure that the day of the one dimensional Black man was on the way out.

I asked him why?

"Mainly because he is boring," he answered.

Taking a Leaf: A Talk with Albert Murray

Marvin Gelfand / 1974

From *West Side Literary Review,* 1, no. 2 (April 25, 1974), p. 3. Reprinted with permission by *The Westsider.*

***Train Whistle Guitar* is your first novel after three books of criticism, essays and reportage—*The Omni-Americans, The Hero and the Blues* and *South to a Very Old Place*—what's next?**

The Blues for Background which will be a history of the idiom and ritual of the blues. Most of my next novel is finished and it carries Scooter (the boy-hero of *Train Whistle*) up through his college years. A third novel will take him to his maturity. I also have a big novel working—700 or so pages in manuscript—with the title *Fifty Roads to Town. The Blues* . . . is a documentary dealing with the ritualistic dimensions of the blues and the circumstance surrounding their extension of a people's consciousness. An art form does give you the soul and spirit of a people and I'm trying to come up with a literary equivalent of that communion of souls . . . a literary equivalent of the blues with which I grew up. What it said and where it was and is said. One chapter for the documentary has the working title "K.C. 4/4 and the Velocity of Celebration"; another is "Concerto for Satch." It all moves toward Ellington who is the Shakespeare of the idiom. I'm going to write about "Duke Ellington as Noun and Verb" . . .

Have literary models influenced your writing as much as the blues and jazz?

Joyce, Faulkner, Mann and Hemingway . . . of course, I use every literary device and form to deal with the rich speech of the people I'm writing about. Each girl in *Train Whistle* is written in a series of choruses . . . in solos . . .an Ellington arrangement of "Sweet Georgia Brown." That works for narration and sequence. The music is the right style for the time. The style is statement. It's the structure for their experience. The contemporary literary mind is very subtle and I play in *Train Whistle Guitar* with the fabulous, with fairytale, memoir, set-piece oration, sermons, shouts. Blues idiom is a context—a framework within which I'm trying to define contemporary heroism. Blues make you confront experience and then you do the riffs. The breaks give you an opportunity, though many are terrified when the music seems to stop; for good dancers that's the time to cut into it and improvise. The blues—if we understand them—can help create an American free and improvisatory life style. They're part of our bravery. Storytellers are blues singers. Jazz musicians do what Shakespeare did with Holinshed's *Chronicles* and Thomas Kyd's tragedies. You can almost hear Will saying: "Burbage, you take trumpet."

None of this sounds very political. Do you get criticized for being too literary, not committed enough?

That's an old story and Harold Cruse handles it beautifully in *The Crisis of the Negro Intellectual.* I'm no spokesman for my people, nor should I be, nor should anyone. Cruse knows, and I know that "Take me to your leader" talk is foolishness because there are too many to be spoken for by anyone and too many who won't let anyone speak their piece for them. If it is chaotic, so be it; that's the sign of freedom and life.

What do you do when you teach young people literature in the universities?

I try to get them to see that accurate metaphor and accurate fable are more dependable than concepts in scientific jargon which are only pseudo-scientific. Wisdom is metaphor . . . images to live by, Kenneth Burke called them. I'll talk about self-realization because that is a perfect American theme and begins in the Constitution and the Declaration. I'll look at Melville's *Benito Cereno* and try to show that Melville is inventing freedom in his own way in that story. Many critics miss that problem of freedom; when they see Negroes they go dumb. Styron in *Nat Turner* fell for the exoticism and "Sambo" theorizing. He missed the "black mask of humanity" that Ellison spoke of. James Baldwin tells people what they already think they know. The schools are too positivistic—social science is the new piety. When I hear a man say rate or per cent, I want to reach for my switchblade. He's into prophecy without knowing it. Well, Baldwin has fallen into the trap of the proletarian novelists. He gives lip-service to the blues—Bessie Smith. But he forgets myth. He's accepting the welfare orientation as his content. I'm talking about heroism and its blues context. Baldwin is too much derivative from Richard Wright. It's what Eliot talked about in "Tradition and the Individual Talent." Artists counterstate what they disagree with and extend what they like. A jazz musician hears a syrupy ballad so he roughs it up—counterstates it. On something from Louie he does extending riffs with love. I don't copy Joyce, note for note, but try to extend.

In *Train Whistle Guitar* I counterstate the conventional black nonsense. For in fact, the kids are/were always taught to be heroic. I counterstate the sociology . . . I extend Mann's Joseph stories, Nick Adams in a story like "In Our Time" and *Portrait of the Artist as a Young Man.* Luzana Cholly, the guitarist, is Odysseus, Beowulf, Roland and all the heroes to Scooter. Auden talked about the "true ancestor" whom you don't find by going back along a straight line. Boys have lots of fathers and the book is about fathers. Those images and metaphor make you see possibilities. Sociologists and sociological novelists only think in terms of force or power or dollars. Their constricted vision of human possibility is undramatic and untrue.

Is it hard to be a literary intellectual now?

I am literary and some say I'm less black because of it but that really means less cliché. Fiction isn't dead . . . there's no death of interest in narrative. People watch stories on the TV. Storytelling and image-making won't die. A specific convention may decline and decay but not the art. The new journalism—quasi-documentary image—only works so long as the guy doing it has a talent for narration. Mailer wins by cheating; he can tell a story better than the average journalist. What's Mailer doing but what Twain did when he had to make money? People who talk about historical breakthroughs don't know history. What do they do that wasn't in *Life on the Mississippi* or in *Walden.*

What do you go out of your way to read now?

Cormac McCarthy is very strong . . . he handles his idiom beautifully and has a great intelligence. I like William Gass and Kozinski's *Painted Bird* and *Steps.* Walker Percy's *The Moviegoer* is for rereading. I'm so busy doing my own stuff I don't have enough time to read around, but I do reread Malraux, Joyce, Faulkner, Eliot and especially the superb Auden. I read my friends' work . . . Penn Warren is always good. Somebody like Pynchon is not to my taste. Roth is gifted but too sociological. He is impaired in that way as Bellow is not. Bellow deals with the texture of life and has humor and irony, for instance the black pickpocket in *Mr. Sammler's Planet* and *Herzog* involved in a traffic accident having two negro cops calling him Moses and enjoying his Jewish discomfort. Bellow has the narrative skill and he's one who knows that images don't change every year like generalizations. Henry James wrote at the same time as Freud did his treatises. Who revises Henry James? I don't think Trilling is right when he says the narrative is dying, though it is painful to see artists getting tricked by current jargon like "ghetto" and "middle class" and other equally empty concepts. They end up saying walking is out of style. I'm interested in continuing the species and not counting orgasms. I have to go back to basic and primitive motives. Man needs form to counteract chaos . . . for chaos leads to hysteria. Narration is such a form.

You don't think much of literary criticism then?

Not when they are too eager to be politically hip, rather than to do what literary critics should, to mediate between works of art and the uninstructed reader. Warren's criticism is always a pleasure to read and Cleanth Brooks also because they take the stories seriously and not some current political orthodoxy.

William Troy, R. P. Blackmur and Kenneth Burke all provide a standard to which young critics should aspire. Good criticism would help black writing which suffers from excessive contemporaneity. Too many writers don't regard themselves as human beings but as political abstractions. Blues are about life; they are a line of continuity and individual vision. The real problem is to make white Americans more aware of the black dimension of their experience. Frederick Douglass and Harriet Tubman are theirs too. Most Black Studies programs were opportunistic and not really carefully thought-out responses to a real academic need. By the way, "Black" is a whiter word than negro . . . and I'm going to write on that soon. Black is loaded, so why pick it? A lot of it is jiving. I'm not a racist. I have Ellington-friends and books-friends; Hemingway-friends and Mann-friends. It's not race and I get angry when someone mouths off about the *BLACK HERITAGE* but can't listen to a 25-year-old Ellington record and gets intimidated by a white guy who plays a 100-year-old thing that's "in" now. James P. Johnson or Eubie Blake were never "out" with me. But it would be bad reporting and bad journalism to put me into a polemical cliche or slot. Equality is scripture and I believe in a kind of Whitmanesque nationalism that Bessie Smith and Fats Waller are a part of. Or Louis Armstrong when he put on his black mask . . . he was a hard, tough man but he performed with that black mask on and then that became the only Satch people knew.

Do you think of yourself as a southern novelist?

Like Percy, Reynolds Price, Ernest Gaines, Faulkner, Cormac McCarthy, Katherine Anne Porter, Eudora Welty or Flannery O'Connor? Yes. A critic should spend time placing me as a southern novelist . . . as much or more than placing me as a black novelist. Mr. Kazin seems to have missed that.

Albert Murray: Riffing It

Beverly Grunwald / 1976

From *Women's Wear Daily,* October 21, 1976, p. 35. Reprinted by permission of Fairchild Publications/*Women's Wear Daily.*

"I'm sort of saying that life is a jam session." Albert Murray was talking to me about his latest book, *Stomping the Blues,* and grinning at his own conclusion.

An intellectual who has gathered the strengths of the great philosophers as well as Mama Hagar and Uncle Remus, Murray is a brilliant social and literary critic with some heavy thoughts that he lightens with devilish humor. He understands black-white relationships like no one I've ever met. Above all, he understands America. He has his own interpretations for the rhythms of life, history and human experience.

Stomping the Blues is a handsome source book for the jazz buff with its vintage photographs and evaluation of heroes like Louis Armstrong, Duke Ellington, Bessie Smith, Jelly Roll Morton, Charlie Parker. But more intriguing is the philosophy expressed by an original thinker—that blues are a frame of reference in which we can define American heroism.

"It boils down to a confrontation of the facts of life, acceptance of life in a precarious situation and riffing or extemporizing on the exigencies of the situation as a musician does in a jam session. Improvisation is the ultimate human skill—the very essence of heroism.

"What I'm dealing with in this book are very fundamental things. The blues as such represent an affliction, something to do with melancholia, depression, gloom. Now blues music is an antidote to the condition of having the blues—and so one plays blues music. And in the process of stomping away the blues, you don't stomp in violence—but with elegance. It's not just raw defiance, there's a certain amount of disdain."

The heroes of *Stomping the Blues* are the key people who Murray feels have refined the ritual into art. He calls the ritual itself "the Saturday night function," as opposed to the Sunday morning service which is a sacred response to the problems of life. "It's a secular response and therefore more available to literature with all its riffs. I submit that art is the ultimate refinement of ritual." As he sees it, the ritual of purification becomes a fertility ritual and, by extension, a celebration.

Beating out a heavy rhythm at our luncheon table, Murray stresses that blues or jazz music is **good-time** music. "The sociological approach or the white folkloric premise talks about misery. I'm talking about enjoyment, of counter-stating misery, about the confrontation of music. The irony is that it's the most joyous music in the world.

"I don't agree with the social scientists," he says. "Moynihan's thesis in *The Negro Family* went as far as to say the guy didn't strut. The whole Negro thing is based on strutting. How could anyone make an evaluation of a culture for official purposes and leave out the most obvious thing? When you see an American Negro walking down the street, he's dancing—in spite of every-thing. But Moynihan is saying he may be broke, he doesn't vote, he doesn't do this or that—he may be awfully depressed. But there's Louis Armstrong's trumpet raised to the top of the Empire State Building and everyone feels better as soon as they hear it. 'I just love that Satch,' they say. Gershwin? You want to find out the importance of Gershwin. But you don't love him."

In previous books, *The Omni-Americans, South to a Very Old Place, The Hero and the Blues,* the provocative author has considered Negro culture and the role of the blacks, racism, slavery, segregation and Southern white "pretty goodness and God awfulness" along with autobiography. A well-read, well-spoken writer who has fantastic recall, Murray believes that a person who has a sense of literature is better able to deal with life's complexities than a mind shaped by political ideas. When he explains this—or anything—it's with a professor's patience—a role he takes on from time to time in between writing.

Who are you voting for? I asked my Alabama-born friend who currently lives in Harlem.

"Carter. I think we should try that. It's a better alternative. We should experiment with Carter because going with Ford is not playing it safe. I'm tired of people saying, 'Good old Jerry.' Jerry is an awful guy. He's never had much feeling for social improvement. He will tolerate all kinds of things. People forget. Ford is now paying for the fact that he was hand-picked by Nixon, pardoned Nixon, is a continuation of Nixon. I think it would be a marvelous Bicentennial gesture to experiment with Carter. It's like what I was dealing with in *South to a Very Old Place*—Lyndon Johnson's South. There's a trust that American Negroes feel. Listen in a black barbershop and you'll hear, "Well, you never know about those Northern guys. They can act nice—but you never know what they're doing behind your back. Whereas if a Southern guy promises you something, you can depend on it. He'll turn over hell and anything else to do it."

Murray was appalled that Ford did not take immediate action on Earl Butz's controversial, obscene anti-black remarks. Then he proceeded to mischievously dissect those remarks. "He's not very hip," he laughed. "The general image is that blacks are indiscriminately promiscuous rather than selective in sex." Regarding the second part—that they like loose shoes— "They wear the neatest shoes in the country. Heck, they're not shoeshine guys for nothing." And, as far as a warm place to relieve themselves, he asserts, "They're not fussy. Butz should see the urine in the streets of Harlem."

On a more serious note, the writer worries about the things that racism does to the well-meaning white intellectual. All blacks are not the same. Sometimes just because the man is black and feels needed, people don't listen to what he is saying. "West Indians think more like other immigrants. But it is a different sensibility from the native black American's," he explains. "They don't know very much about this country and they're not very involved. They go basically on abstractions. Like Africans. When you're talking to them, most of the time you're talking to Marxists. Colonial Marxists.

"One of the things I celebrate about American Negroes is that they came out of slavery with their humanity intact. There was no hope for them but they found hope for human life. Not in the sense of exercising power by arrogance, which is what most people mean by freedom. They came out with a fine orientation to native cuisine, with a sex life that is the envy of Earl Butz; they came out with the laughter that's infectious—all these things are very important."

Murray pooh-poohs the whole African heritage exploration fuss. A 20th-Century American, he sees no point in learning Swahili, Afro haircuts and quaint costumes. He is not about to go sifting for his African ancestors like Alex Haley in *Roots.*

"For my purpose I go back to 1619 or whenever it was that cargo of the first 20 blacks was dropped in Virginia. Once they came here, they became Americans and you had the birth of the blues—let us say—which the Africans have no connection with. The essence of the black experience in America is in that art form, that idiom which is blues music. African music doesn't vary. They don't riff."

And for Albert Murray, riffing is what it's all about.

Albert Murray Talks the Blues

Jason Berry / 1976

From *Southern Booklore,* 1977, pp. 12–13. Reprinted by permission of Caroline Harkleroad for *Southern Booklore* and Jason Berry.

Alabama born Albert Murray is one of the most original writers in America today. A distinguished jazz and literary critic, his first novel was published in 1974, *Train Whistle Guitar,* and won the Lillian Smith Award for best Southern novel. Murray is also the author of the highly acclaimed *The Omni-Americans, South to a Very Old Place* and *The Hero and the Blues,* but many feel that his most ambitious book to date is *Stomping the Blues.* Both *Train Whistle Guitar* and *Stomping the Blues* draw on blues and jazz music in a dazzling stream of consciousness based on *sounds.* In *Train Whistle,* Murray used this style to tell of a young boy's experience in Alabama during the Depression. In *Stomping* it is used as an interpretation of blues music as an expression of a race and culture. Sample:

And yet the irrepressible joyousness, the downright exhilaration, the rapturous delight in sheer physical existence, like the elegant jocularity and hearty nonsense that are no less characteristic of blues music, are unsurpassed by any other dance music in the world. Still, the captivating elegance that always seems so entirely innate to blues-idiom dance movement is something earned in a context of antagonism. Not unlike the parade-ground oriented sporty limp walk of the epic hero and the championship athlete, it has been achieved through the manifestations of such grace under pressure as qualifies the matador, for example, for his suit of lights and his pigtail.

Murray writes lucidly of the Saturday Night Function; the sounds and meanings conveyed by railroads; ironic condemnations of religious ministers in churches where the faithful swing and sway, in movement not far removed from down-home blues stomping. An entire chapter is devoted to correcting misconceptions about the blues, and the connotations of blues in American culture.

Stomping the Blues is also one of the most handsomely illustrated books of music history ever published. Murray undoubtedly spent long hours gathering rare photographs of Louis Armstrong, Bessie Smith, and others; his

15

captions often contain valuable information about sidemen, musicians who played in bands but were previously unheralded.

Albert Murray here talks the blues with me:

JB: Black fiction stems from a largely realist tradition. Your novel and recent non-fiction books are written in a lyrical, indeed musical style. Do you consider this a departure from the realist tradition?

AM: I am searching for an adequate metaphor or "objective correlative" for my conception of contemporary actuality. Realism, regardless of academic definitions, is essentially only a literary device among other literary or narrative devices—no less than naturalism, fantasy, surrealism and so on. Yes, in a sense I suppose you can say that many U.S. Negro writers have relied on "realistic" devices. But it seems to me that they have mostly been preoccupied with the literal document as agit-prop journalism, so much so that for all the realistic details to make the reader feel *that all this really happened,* their stories seldom rise above the level of one-dimensional patently partisan social case histories. The Afro-U.S. tradition of idiomatic storytelling on the other hand (not unlike others elsewhere) is largely concerned with the exploits of epic heroes who are involved with the complexities of human motives and with the contradictions of human nature and with the ultimate inscrutability of nature as such.

JB: In line with that, I wonder if there are any other novelists today doing the same kind of innovative fiction—and non-fiction—that you're doing, imbuing jazz rhythms into fiction and prose?

AM: There is Ellison of course, and there are others that I like for one reason or another, but as of now I am unaware of any others who share either his or my involvement with the blues as a literary device. Over the years there has been a tendency to confuse the blues with folk expression. Where the hell did U.S. Negro writers get the idea that folk, which is to say peasant or provincial, art (or artlessness) is adequate to the complexities of black experience in contemporary America? Louis knew better than that and so did Jelly Roll and Papa Joe and Duke, and they extended that folk stuff as far as talent and craft enabled them.

JB: I've long felt that the English epic poem, which grew into the novel, was in many ways an extension of the ballad. In America there doesn't seem to be much of a musical underpinning to our literature—I guess because our literature was borrowed, historically speaking, from England. Do you think many critics today are receptive to, or aware of, the changes going on in black fiction?

AM: I'm not so sure that the English novel is as directly derived from the epic and the ballad as you suggest. Perhaps some influence of poetry was inevitable, but a much more obvious source seems to have been the old practice of diary and journal keeping and letter writing. Nor do I think American literature was borrowed from English literature. It is rather an extension of English language and literature. Also, I don't know how far you can take that musical underpinnings business. What about Melville and Mark Twain? It seems to me that the oral tradition out of which they worked had musical underpinnings. Man, those old New England preachers were not only musical as hell but they are also the major source for the downhome pulpit style and manner. There are Afro elements in most downhome things, to be sure; but what they represent is an Afro dimension or Afro accent which sometimes adds up to an idiom—but—an idiom within an existing tradition or convention. (As with basketball, if you get what I mean. The game is from the Midwest, but idiomatically it is more and more an extension of downhome and uptown choreography.) But back to your point, Joyce's work was obviously influenced by Irish poetry and music, but Gertrude Stein was not less preoccupied with the music inherent in language as such. Critics? Man, most critics seem to feel that unless you are pissing and moaning about injustice you have nothing to say. In any case it seems that they find it much easier to praise black (brown and beige) writers for being angry (which requires no talent, not to mention genius) than for being innovative.

JB: I'm fascinated with the influence of Hemingway on your work. In one article you say that his heroes are blues heroes, which makes a lot of sense. But your style and his are quite different. In what stylistic sense, if any, has he influenced you?

AM: Hemingway writes a prose that strikes you as being realistic and is indeed more accurate than most reportage but is at the very same time the very essence of ritual. His cadence is that of process and of ritual reenactment as well. As casual as it seems, his style achieves its realistic effect through incantation.

JB: Lastly, and I hope you don't horselaugh when I say this, but would you consider yourself a romantic?

AM: I most certainly do not regard myself as being romantic in any academic sense that suggests Byron, Shelley, Keats and Wordsworth. On the other hand take a look at *The Hero and the Blues.* Look at the very last paragraph. In view of what we now think we know about the physical nature of the universe, anybody who thinks of human life as a story is romantic. The thing to avoid is sentimentality. To struggle against the odds, to continue in the face of adversity is romantic, which is to say, heroic. To protest the existence of dragons (or even Grand Dragons for that matter) is not only sentimental but naive, or so it seems to me.

Albert Murray: Up Tempo or "The Velocity of Celebration"

Beverly Bateman / 1978

From *Off Peachtree,* 1, no. 8 (September 1978), pp. 40–41. Reprinted with the gracious permission of Beverly Bateman Trater.

This interview was conducted in Atlanta during the spring of 1978, when Mr. Murray was writer-in-residence at Emory University.

"The jam session was not primarily an experimental workshop; it was to remain essentially the same old multidimensional good-time after-hour gathering it had always been. The experimental innovations were mainly a matter of having something special to strut your stuff with when your turn came to solo on the riff-solo-riff merry-go-round" (Albert Murray in *Stomping the Blues*).

Albert Murray orchestrates the conversation—and it's not just a sedate talk on a summer's hot afternoon. It's a dance, an up-tempo jam session, a dialogue with the sun in the sky or a jar full of honeysuckle on a desk, and anything else within reach of gesture, or a leap of the mind. His ideas are expressed in the form of vamps, riffs, breaks, choruses and out-choruses. In fact, Murray often speaks of his writing as an attempt to create the literary equivalent of jazz composition.

The Vamp: "Sometimes it all begins with the piano player vamping till ready, a vamp being an improvised introduction" *(Stomping the Blues)*.

Murray, this year's writer in residence at Emory University, was born in Nokomis, Alabama, in 1916. That Southern childhood is the concern of his beautifully received novel *Train Whistle Guitar* (1974). The things that grew out of that childhood—music, philosophy, politics, literature—have been the passions of his life and the concern of most of his work. A retired major in the Air Force, Murray has lived in, been published by and lectured at a long list of places. His non-fiction works include *The Omni-Americans* (1970), *South to a Very Old Place* (1971), *The Hero and the Blues* (1973) and *Stomping the Blues* (1976). At the moment, he's completing a second novel to be called *The Spyglass Tree,* in the trilogy which began with *Train Whistle Gui-*

tar; he's collaborating with Count Basie on that gentleman's autobiography; and finishing a sequel to *The Hero and the Blues.*

Murray writes and talks about the music, philosophy, politics, literature, and life he lives. It's all the same fine tune, played with elegance and sophistication in four/four by Andy Kirk's Clouds of Joy out of Kansas City—played in heroic affirmation at what Murray calls "the velocity of celebration." Or, as Duke Ellington wrote, "Albert Murray is a man whose learning did not interfere with understanding . . . He is the unsquarest person I know."

The Riff: "A blues riff is a brief musical phrase that is repeated, sometimes with very subtle variations, over the length of a stanza as the chordal pattern follows its normal progression . . . When they are effective, riffs always seem as spontaneous as if they were improvised in the heat of performance. So much so that riffing is sometimes regarded as being synonymous with improvisation" *(Stomping the Blues).*

Music, philosophy, politics, literature—Murray has been riffing on one theme, the theme of any good storyteller, the theme of heroism. "Yeah, well, that brings up the concept which I discuss in *The Hero and the Blues* as antagonistic cooperation. In the fairy tale, for example, if you didn't have the dragon, you couldn't have the hero . . . So the heroic attitude that I am concerned with precisely, is how one continues in the face of adversity. And that's one of the interesting things about the blues idiom frame of reference, as I have been trying to develop it philosophically and apply it as a writer. The whole thing develops or is designed to condition one to regard a disjuncture or some frustrating force as an opportunity. So that in jazz, or in a blues composition, the break is precisely that point at which the musician improvises or creates, and that to me is the essence of heroic action."

The Break: "Another technical device peculiar to blues music is the break, which is a very special kind of ad-lib passage or cadenza-like interlude between two musical phrases that are separated by an interruption or interval in the established cadence" *(Stomping the Blues).*

"Obstacles are what creativity is about. You know, solving problems, confronting and transcending difficulties, that kind of thing is the essence of struggle or *agon.* All stories, every drama, is a matter of the struggle. Without that cooperative antagonism you wouldn't have creativity. The dragon must exist for the hero to do his thing, right?"

There's the dragon of political injustice: "It's a challenge, it would seem to me. You know, I'm not primarily a political commentator . . . The hero concept can be translated into anything. Someone has to confront the political circumstances and spell them out. I was concerned about that sort of thing in my first book, *The Omni-Americans,* because I saw misdefinitions and I knew that the policies for corrective action would be inadequate. Counterstatement does not have to be simplified into just protest, polemical protest." Murray's powerful counterstatement was an affirmative battlehymn sung against the misdirected shouts of black separatists and the inept moanings of social scientists. Ralph Ellison, among others, called the work "indispensable."

"It's the quality of the dialogue at a given moment. We can look at it as a jam session. When I wrote *The Omni-Americans,* I took a voice, literally the mask, of a piano player. And I said all these guys are blowing these solos and they've forgotten what the basic chords are. You know, what is the nature of humanity and experience? What is the nature of American experience? I want affirmation. The artist is concerned with the terms on which he will survive as a human being.

"I listened to and participated in the dialogue of the 1960s. People from all quarters were saying things which violated not only my sense of the idiom in which I lived, but my sense of what human nature is."

As Murray writes in *The Hero and the Blues,* "In effect, protest or finger-pointing fiction such as *Uncle Tom's Cabin* and *Native Son,* addresses itself to the humanity of the dragon in the very process of depicting him as a fire-snorting monster: 'Shame on you, Sir Dragon,' it says in effect, 'be a nice man and a good citizen.' (Or is it, 'Have mercy, Massa?')"

"So the sociologists were all out in left field, as if they'd never seen a human being in their lives. People with their infinite pretentiousness would keep on picking up the terminology and repeating it, without relating it to everyday experiences. The statements the sociologists and the survey-technicians were making, and the spokesmen were taking up, were violating my basic conception of how everything works.

"Of course, if we have an automobile and it runs out of gas, well, it stops; but a hungry human being may be motivated to do something which he would not do if his stomach were full. The empty tank analogy which was being woven into the rhetoric of the '60s was the rhetoric of Marxist revolution. They had good motives. They were violating life and complicating a problem. The motives were—'Well, if we make people dissatisfied, then they will rebel.' They just had one conception of how to have a revolution. What they were doing was picturing the masses to themselves as hopelessly lost. How you going to have a revolution with that? I'm just too radical to go for that

kind of conservatism. If you're talking about revolution, you better go looking for some potential heroes or some heroic potential."

The quest: Murray came to Atlanta in the early '70s to talk with fellow
knight-errants like Ralph McGill, to forge a few swords and slay a few dragons. He writes of the journey in *South to a Very Old Place: "In all events
you have picked up the* Harper's *Magazine advance against expenses and are
enroute south, this time not as a reporter as such and even less as an ultra
gung-ho black spokesman but rather as a Remus-derived, book-oriented
downhome boy (now middle-aged) with the sort of Alabama buster brown-
hip (you hope) curiosity 'that implies impression that knits knowledge that
finds the name-form that whets the wits that convey contacts that sweeten
sensation that drives desire that adheres to attachment that dogs death that
bitches birth that entails the ensuance of existentiality.' If you could get
enough of all that together you were pretty certain that all of the required
polemics would also be there as a matter of course."*

He speaks of his political writings, "It was a matter of doing for the experience what other people have done for other experiences, of achieving what
we would call *in the language of the day."* He laughs at the pretentious
terminology of that language, " 'a viable synthesis,' that is, something which
is truly practical. You got to understand context to understand details." The
also . . .

The Riff: "But then in the jam session, which seems to have been the
direct source of the Kansas City riff style as featured by Bennie Moten, Count
Basie, and Andy Kirk, among others, improvisation includes spontaneous
appropriation . . . no less than on-the-spot invention . . . The invention or
creative process lies not in the originality of the phrase as such, but in the
way it is used in a frame of reference!" *(Stomping the Blues).*

In *Train Whistle Guitar,* Murray riffs on the Orphic image of guitar player
Luzanna Cholly's sporty-limp-walk, which Scooter, the novel's small protagonist in training for the heroic life, tries to imitate: *"Because the also and
also of all that was also the also plus also of so many of the twelve-bar
twelve-string guitar riddles you got whether in idiomatic iambics or otherwise mostly from Luzanna Cholly who was the one who used to walk his
trochaic-sporty stomping-ground limp-walk picking and plucking and
knuckle knocking and strumming (like an anapestic locomotive) while sing-
songsaying Anywhere I hang my hat anywhere I prop my feet. Who could
drink muddy water who could sleep in a hollow log."*

The Break: "Indeed the improvisation on the break, which is required of blues-idiom musicians and dancers alike, is precisely what epic heroism is based on . . . It is not at all unusual for one musician's break to become another's riff chorus—or lead melody" *(Stomping the Blues)*.

The break, of course, is also what civilization is based on. "Now, if a person gives the impression that you cannot possibly be creative, write a book, make a painting, compose music unless you have three hot meals a day and have a warm place to live in, he's counterstating all the biographies of artists that I've ever read. This is just plain stupid . . . That sporty-limp-walk means you're going to get hurt. The suffering is subtly built in there . . .

"The break is as much an opportunity for heroism as a source of trauma. The artist has to have a certain openness to experience, a certain knowledge that life has always to be improvised; but it has to be improvised out of a knowledge of chordal structure and progression that is as rich as you can make it. The more tunes you have in your background, the better prepared to improvise you are."

The Dance: "Blues music, however, is neither negative nor sentimental. It counterstates the torch singer's sob story, sometimes as if with the snap of two fingers! What the customary blues-idiom dance movement reflects is a disposition to encounter obstacle after obstacle as a matter of course. Such jive expressions as *getting with it* and *taking care of business* are references to heroic action" *(Stomping the Blues)*.

Murray likes to walk around the room as he talks. "This whole business of objectifying human consciousness probably first took shape in the form of the gesture, which became the dance, and, of course, that's basic reenactment of the survival techniques of a given time and place. Language is probably a more sophisticated extension of this."

"Jazz reviewers and commentators who place primary emphasis on concert hall music almost always seem to forget what is actually being stylized," states Murray. "They seem oblivious to the ritual without which there would be no art. The real basis for understanding any art form is the underlying ritual. Blues, or jazz, is no exception."

Murray must know that his own life embodies style—stomps, jumps, and swings style. "You have the void. You have chaos. You have entropy, the tendency of all phenomena to become random. That's just raging chaos and, of course, that's what the villain signifies in fiction, what the dragon signifies and so forth. Now it's not by force alone that one conquers chaos—that one conquers the dragon. It's style that one uses to do that. It's elegance. It's a refinement of insight and it's a matter of choreographing the movement in

order to counteract force with style. And generally when we talk about freedom, we mean our style is cramped."

The Out-Chorus: A little later, when the sun's gone down, Murray speaks
to a filled auditorium, but first plays some records by way of introduction:
He plays Jelly Roll Morton, with The Red Hot Peppers riffing on "The Kansas City Stomp." Everyone sits cramped in their seats and a few are radical
enough to snap a finger, or unembarrassed enough to tap a foot. It's a room
filled with people wishing they were heroic enough to rise up, to slay dragons
and blue devils . . . to dance.

To Hear Another Language

Alvin Ailey, James Baldwin, Romare Bearden,
and Albert Murray / 1978

From *Callaloo,* 12, no. 3 (Summer 1989), pp. 431–52. © 1989, The
Johns Hopkins University Press. Reprinted with permission.

The transcription of this conversation, filmed and recorded for the documentary *Bearden Plays Bearden* (Third World Cinema Productions,
Inc.), was edited by Nelson E. Breen.

On December 15, 1978, four longtime friends, Romare Bearden, Alvin Ailey,
Albert Murray, and James Baldwin, gathered at the home of the art publisher,
Hugh McKay. From the filmmaker's point-of-view, the location was ideal: a
beautiful apartment with a wood burning fireplace; high ceilings; a balcony
overlooking the livingroom (for high angle shots); a magnificent collection
of original works by the likes of Chagall, Picasso, Miro, and Vassarely; and
Bearden's new prints from his "ODYSSEY" collages. In addition, the colors
and textures of the apartment were perfect extensions of Bearden's paintings.

Our initial production plan to film Romare in separate one hour conversations with Messrs. Baldwin, Ailey, and Murray was enhanced by the simultaneous arrival of these notable gentlemen at Mr. McKay's—a streak of good
fortune for the production team. We knew we would be on a tight schedule,
but the impact of that moment had to be captured. So much for plans. Baldwin was traveling down from Massachusetts (where he was finishing his latest
novel). We assured him that he would be required to stay no longer than an
hour. The same assurance applied to Ailey, whose ballet company was then
near the end of its run at City Center, and he was required to be at a rehearsal
that afternoon.

Briefly, they asked the normal intimate questions that lapses of time re-
quire between friends; they hugged each other and joked. Then they sat down
by the fireplace and, with two cameras running, began a dialogue that was to
last more than four hours.

Filmmaking is largely an endeavor in intangibles. On this particular afternoon, we had the privilege of witnessing four men who are giants of contemporary culture coming together to eloquently and passionately express their

25

remembrances, feelings, and insights on a wide variety of themes, all connected by their relationship to Bearden's work and life.

What follows are excerpts of their discussions. Initially, the conversation turned to Paris in the 1950s, and the days spent together by Bearden, Baldwin, and Murray. Eventually, their talk jumps backwards and forwards, in time and place, and expands our perceptions of the cultural, historical, political and social history of America in the twentieth century.

Above all, it examines how these four men, and Bearden in particular, processed their experiences into unique and original statements within the universal context of art.

This segment consists of material that is largely personal and anecdotal. It invokes a Paris where, in Romare's phrase, "Life was lived in the streets." For Bearden, Baldwin and Murray, it was a time of coming to terms with their conditions as black Americans so that they could come to terms with their art. And for Romare, in particular, it provided an exciting sense of community that recalled Harlem in the 20s and 30s, where writers, painters, musicians and intellectuals constantly exchanged ideas and experiences.

Bearden: Here we are with some great friends of mine, Albert Murray, James Baldwin and Alvin Ailey. This is a great day for me.

Baldwin: It's a great day for us, Romie.

Murray: Always happy to re-encounter old buddies.

Bearden: That's right. Jimmy's here from Paris. You remember Paris?

Baldwin: Yes, I remember Paris.

Bearden: I was telling Alvin that you invited me to lunch one day. Jimmy had this little place, he invited about twenty or thirty people, and he had the biggest frying pan that I've ever seen and nothing but potatoes. You remember that? Everybody thought that it was just wonderful.

Baldwin: That was a long time ago.

Bearden: That was a long time ago and you were writing *Go Tell It on the Mountain.* You hadn't finished it. Don't you remember?

Murray: It was called, *I, John.*

Baldwin: I was calling it, *I, John.* That's right. Yes, I met you at the same time.

Murray: That was the summer of 1950.

Bearden: Where did you get that skillet?

Baldwin: I don't know. I think I got it from a Corsican lady. I got it in very doubtful, dubious ways. We were living by wits in Paris then. For a long time I had the biggest room in the quarter—the biggest hotel room.

Bearden: When I met you, you had moved from the big room to this small one.

Baldwin: Yes.

Bearden: He had invited all those people.

Baldwin: You know where that was. That was in St. Sulpice.

Bearden: That's where I did the murals in the church. You ever been there, Al?

Murray: Yeah, I visited Jimmy over there. I met Jimmy and Romie that summer. Romie had already been a friend of another old friend of ours, Ralph Ellison. I had met him in Harlem. I met Romie in Paris that summer. And of course, I met you when you came up to Kaplan's.

Baldwin: That's right, I met you there.

Murray: At a dinner party.

Bearden: You took over his apartment?

Murray: Well, his wife went home and he invited some people to live up there. Lionel Abel, and an Italian painter named Sabetelli. We had parties there and musicians in there.

Baldwin: You tore up Montparnasse, in fact.

Murray: Yes, we did. Roy Eldridge came and played and then Minta Cato was there at the party one night.

Baldwin: That's right, I remember that very well.

Murray: You remember I was trying to stop them from singing "Indian Love Call"? We were trying to swing them away from Victor Herbert things.

Bearden: And we invited them to this party. When we got there I heard this jazz music. They said, "This is not Frenchmen." So we went up there . . . it was Roy Eldridge, Sidney Bechet and Minta Cato. We brought them to the party. We got so loud the police came and then we had to do the party out into the streets. You know Minta Cato was married at one time to Andy Razaf—he used to write lyrics for Fats Waller. She was over there at that time and that's when you had invited me and a whole gang of people to St. Sulpice when you had that big frying pan. You could fry a person in that frying pan.

Baldwin: We were all by definition more or less illiterate because we had never been to Europe before. And, some of those people had ties to Europe that we could not claim. . . . It was kind of fascinating to be endlessly instructed, if you see what I mean. You really were being instructed in a way that no one else . . . in a way that the heirs of Europe could not imagine that you were being instructed.

Bearden: Jimmy, you used to move.

Baldwin: Oh baby, I moved.

Bearden: What I meant was that when I would be sitting down, Jimmy was going here and there and—what was that cafe, the La Reine Blanche?

Baldwin: La Reine Blanche, the one on St. Germaine.

Bearden: He had a certain thing here, here and he was moving. "Hello? How are you?"

Murray: This is the heyday of St. Germaine-des-Pres. We usually could find Jimmy in La Mabillon.

Baldwin: La Mabillon is where the dregs of Paris gathered. But they were very beautiful dregs, you know.

Murray: They had moved a sort of floating crap game from the San Remo in the Village.

Bearden: I had my studio and three meals a day for $37.50 a month. It was a little bit more for "chauffage"—heat—in the winter. The concierge said, "Get yourself a nice girl, and she'll heat you up."

Ailey: What were you painting in those days? What kind of things were you doing?

Bearden: The first word I learned in French, Alvin, was *tabare,* which is the word for easel. I went and bought an easel and I didn't do anything because Paris at that time was the wrong place to go if you wanted to find yourself. There was so much to do; it was so easy. You remember I used to know someone at the American Embassy. I think that for $10.50 you got five or seven bottles of any kind of whiskey you wanted. You would go to this person and get these, and we had a party all the time.

Ailey: You didn't do any work?

Bearden: No, we didn't do any work. That was impossible. Jimmy did; I couldn't.

Baldwin: I never went to the American Embassy for reasons I never bothered to figure out.

Murray: To the average person, the Embassy was the American Express.

Bearden: I was on the GI bill and had to go there to be paid.

Baldwin: Well, that makes a difference.

Ailey: How long did you stay in Paris, Romie?

Bearden: Well, it was a couple of years, but when you got paid you never wanted to miss going to the American Embassy on the payday. There was a girl who lived with mice in her hair. Do you remember her?

Baldwin: Yes, I'm afraid I do.

Bearden: She ran out and she kept the mice in her hair. There were all these people who were studying with Isadora Duncan's brother, Raymond Duncan. They were all dressed like Greeks and Romans in these togas and they all came to get their checks—it was just fantastic. You got there early in the morning and stayed there till evening. You really had a sight. Jimmy was there with Richard Wright. Well, those are the last of the great days in Paris. It isn't the same now.

Ailey: Romie, I was wondering how much work you had gotten done in Paris in those days, in the 50s. Jimmy worked but you didn't work.

Bearden: No, I couldn't.

Ailey: Well, what were you doing? Partying?

Bearden: That's right. And, the Chez Inez was . . . everything . . .

Baldwin: But, he was discovering something—partying and discovering something.

Murray: Well, I think that a lot was happening.

Bearden: Inez Cavanaugh was a black singer and she used to write for the *Amsterdam News.* She was married to a Dane, Alvin, named Baron (he was a real baron) Timmy Rosenkrantz. So, Jimmy was there, you were there, and we went there all the time. One time I went there but in the back of it (we didn't know) there was a Chinese gentleman who owned the whole place. He had his cabin in the back. I used to smoke in those days. I was smoking Gauloises and ran out. So, Inez said, "Give Romie a cigarette"; but I didn't know this man gave me hashish. So I smoked two or three things of hashish and I didn't know where I was. Someone told me to walk to the Seine, and I did. I was looking across the Seine and I saw an angel walk across the Seine. So I wanted to become a Catholic. I ran and grabbed her and said, "I confess my sins."

Ailey: It was a female angel?

Bearden: The female angel walked across the Seine. So then, she disappeared and I couldn't find this angel. I went up, and it was about two or three in the morning; there was a lady of the evening there and she said, "What's the matter with you?" I said, "I saw a wonderful thing; an angel walked across the Seine and I can't find her." She said, "I'm no angel, but why don't you go home with me?" She said, "You men are all alike." I said, "What do you mean?" She said, "Look at Notre Dame. You see these angels that are holding the Cathedral up?" And, I said, "Yes." She said, "Don't you think they get tired and want to take a little walk at night? And you're making a whole big thing of this." That was the one painting I wanted to do. The angel walking across the Seine.

Ailey: Did you ever do it?

Bearden: She ruined it for me. I couldn't do that painting.

Ailey: This angel doesn't appear in any later works?

Bearden: No, I just can't do it. I just can't do that painting—that angel walking across the Seine. I'll let you do that as a ballet.

Ailey: Hey, Romy, the thing I'd like to know, not having been in Paris, I think I was in Los Angeles at that time—in Los Angeles City College—what was it like being in Paris and not looking like a black man? In the 50s . . . I mean what was all the feeling and everything else . . . what did the French say?

Bearden: Well, it was a disadvantage . . . to me . . . because I didn't get all the Swedish girls that came down because I didn't look black. Al, you got over. The girls were after you. What did they say to you? [Laughter]

Murray: We were all good friends. . . . Well, Romie did look somewhat Russian. [Laughter] You know, you also looked like Genet. I saw him around and I would see him day after day. He was with Myron O'Higgins. Myron was always a little low-keyed, and Myron was telling his jokes and all of a sudden Romie broke out laughing. He was laughing and started sucking his breath in through his teeth with his tongue in his teeth, you know, a typical Bearden laugh, I found out later, and I said, "Oh, that guy's from Harlem."

Ailey: So Romie, you were not able to paint during the 50s?

Bearden: No, I couldn't paint. Jimmy could write.

Ailey: Were you writing then, Al?

Murray: I was thinking and I had written some stuff which profited from my thinking about it from there. I was operating quite deliberately on the sort of dynamics that I had been reading about.

Ailey: I mean, being in France in the 50s, were you able to write, were you able to absorb?

Murray: Yes, I got a perspective on the American experience which I hadn't had before. I could pull it together—a simple thing like penetrating a menu in a restaurant and realizing what they were saying. You would take all of that hoity toity stuff off and realize what they were talking about. This is the gravy that they make in such-and-such. . . . You suddenly realized how it really worked. What the dynamics of processing everyday elements of culture into fine art, what that happened to be. I could see then down-home cooking in terms of the concept of cuisine. That's great. You can charge a lot of money for that. Many of the restaurants in Paris were trying to get to the preparation of certain things—the way they did it where it was actually grown. They could actually do it like the people who grew it. Any number of things like that were taking place in my mind as a premise of fiction, of history, of culture and that type of thing. So, things were coming together and Jimmy and I were talking about things.

Bearden: And Jimmy was writing *Go Tell It on the Mountain.*

Baldwin: I was writing *Go Tell It on the Mountain.*

Bearden: At that time, his first novel. But, you had a lot of essays.

Baldwin: I wrote a lot of essays before I left the country. What Al is talking about is absolutely true because, in fact, to decipher—that's what you did when you looked at the menus. The bread and butter—how in the world are you going to survive? How do you order what turns out to be a pork chop? And, what is this man saying? If you're an American writer, if you're not Hemingway, but an American black writer in Paris, you live, I lived in a real silence, a real vacuum. But, I was absolutely active because in that silence I began to hear another language; began to hear French and I began to decipher it, in a way, which allowed me to go back (this is what we spent the summer talking about really), which allowed me to hear my father and behind my father, my grandmother and the church I came out of and the pulpit I had just left. At that moment in my life, certainly, all of those things were at once too present, too menacing and too, by paradox therefore, too inaccessible, to get back to where I had been before I was seven years old. I could not do it in the streets where I was running trucks for the garment center. I was living in a kind of limbo in Paris, not exactly limbo, but. . . .

Murray: At the same time, you had to come to terms, I would think (I know from my particular emphasis, I was doing it), with the fact that the church could be the main vehicle of culture that you used for fine art.

Baldwin: But I only began to suspect that that summer.

Murray: That's what I'm saying, it gave you a context, a little perspective.

In this section, the conversation returns to America and Bearden's studio on West 125th Street. He recounts an encounter, almost an epiphany, with a broken-down prostitute that was to have profound effects on his perception of the nature of art. The talk expands to a review of the tradition of creative expression that, for these black Americans, had its roots in the church, a tradition processed and manifested in the music of Duke Ellington, Bessie Smith and Louis Armstrong.

There is also a brief excerpt describing the importance of the WPA during the Depression and how it served to create new opportunities of growth for Americans, especially black American artists.

Ailey: Well, what I really want to know about is Jacob Lawrence and the brown sheet of paper. I mean, your first studio, in Harlem, on 125th Street. You came back from Paris, and you had not painted in Paris. You came back; you had a kind of nervous breakdown. What happened?

Bearden: This was before.

Ailey: You had a nervous breakdown before you went to Paris?

Bearden: No, after. But, this is before, and I had a studio at 33 W. 125th Street that Jacob found for us for $8.00 a month and free electricity. It costs $8.00 a day now if you're lucky.

Ailey: Were you able to work there?

Bearden: No, I had this huge brown sheet of paper.

Ailey: Wrapping paper?

Bearden: Right, because it was cheap, you know, rather than canvas. It stayed there day after day. Claude McKay was in front of me and Jacob Lawrence was downstairs. So, I was coming down this street one day. . . .

Ailey: This is at 33 W. 125th?

Bearden: Yes. There was the homeliest looking woman I had ever seen in my life. She was down there—the women used to have keys 'cause this was in the height of the Depression.

Ailey: These women were standing on the streets?

Bearden: Standing on the street, shaking these keys, which told you what profession they were in. And, we looked at her. "Jesus Christ!" we said, "this woman." She said, "Gentlemen, two dollars"; then she said, "A dollar, fifty cents, a quarter, but for God's sake, please take me." So I went to my mother and I said, "You know, mother, I know the lady is a nice lady, but she's in the wrong profession, could you find a job for her?" And, my mother found a job for this lady. She felt she owed me something. She came and cleaned my studio every Saturday.

Ailey: Were you living in the studio, as well?

Bearden: No, I was living at home but I came to the studio all the time, but I couldn't really work. I remember a fellow had left a turtle there. He had two turtles, one named Abercrombie and one named Fitch. He left Abercrombie with me. Abercrombie used to come out every night, and I thought the turtle—you know how egocentric artists are—I thought it was because he liked my painting. I did a few turtle paintings, but that was about all in those days, in tempera. But, I couldn't do myself. This lady, she saw this brown paper day after day when she came to clean. She said, "Romie, is this the same brown paper I saw last week and all those weeks before?" I said, "Yes, I'm trying to get my mind together." She said, "You know, you told me that I was in the wrong profession." She said, "I got some news for you," and the way I looked at her, she said, "Why don't you paint me?" She wasn't like Miss America or anything to me in those days. She could see from my look how I felt. She said to me, "When you can look into me and find what is beautiful, you'll be able to paint something." This was the greatest lesson in painting I've ever had in my life. Because it isn't the Mona Lisa. You know, everybody talks about how beautiful she is, but no one talks about how beautiful Leonardo da Vinci was. (Or anyone that you translate these things into.) This lady gave me a lesson in painting—like Eugene, earlier in my life—this woman got me to work.

Ailey: I owe a lot to black women in my life. It's very interesting. I understand your mother had a salon.

Bearden: Yes. I'm gonna have my cousin Eddie talk about that. But, this woman did so much for me.

Ailey: Did you paint her?

Bearden: No, I didn't paint her, unfortunately. Maybe the spirit of her is in some paintings, but she gave me a direction, Alvin, in which to move. You know all about that because this is the ritual, this is the thing, and this is your masterpiece.

Ailey: Yes, the Church, I deal with the Church.

Bearden: Revelations of the Blues, see what I mean?

Ailey: But we all do.

Bearden: Somebody said to me, you know, "We have no tradition." We do, we have a definite tradition that comes out of Duke and Bessie Smith and Louis Armstrong. Jimmy's prose is formed out of the Bible or at least the rhythms. . . .

Ailey: Yeah, what was it like to live with Countee Cullen and Langston Hughes, Claude McKay and Inez Cavanaugh? What was it like being a part of that whole big mixture, was that influential? Did it urge you to . . . did it confuse you? Were they such stars that they couldn't accept you?

Bearden: No, no, no. They were very wonderful people and we had a community.

Ailey: Langston Hughes, for example. . . .

Bearden: Langston and Countee were all part of a definite community and you could walk down 7th Avenue . . . you too then, Jimmy?

Baldwin: No, no.

Bearden: You could walk down 7th Avenue and see James Weldon Johnson, Langston, or Countee—all those people were there. You could walk in and they were very accessible.

Ailey: Were these people around for you, Al, too?

Murray: No, I wasn't here, I was in the South.

Ailey: Mobile?

Murray: Mobile and Tuskegee. But, the interesting thing for me—what I discovered when I met Romie in Paris and that was symbolic of the whole relationship—was that it was already operating in a larger context for me.

Ailey: Romie was in Paris, so he wasn't painting.

Murray: Oh, he painted before. He had a lot of stuff. But, the point I'm making is if one talked about Langston Hughes, you know, all the people from the Renaissance period, that's one thing . . . and I had had all that. I grew up with that as an elementary school kid and a high school kid in Mobile because there was never a time when we didn't have what is known as "Black Studies" in the South. By the time I realized that I wanted to be a literary apprentice, that seemed a little bit restrictive for me. It seemed too narrow a view; it didn't seem comprehensive enough; it didn't seem "hip" enough; it did not seem to deal with the larger world that I was already aware of. It seemed a little bit too provincial for me, as much as it meant for me, indispensable as it was. So, I wanted to move beyond that myself and I was looking at problems in art, in literature. I had discovered Sheldon Cheney's *Primer of Modern Art,* and I had heard about Cubism and all that. I had discovered expressionism in the theatre. I knew about Isadora Duncan and all these people; and I was very much interested in the larger context.

When I met Romie, I didn't associate him with the type of thing that was as close to a "folk" or a protest as such. You had these two things that were very prominent with the other writers. All of this was a natural part of his sensibility, but there was a larger thing, and there was never a time when I couldn't talk to Romie about whatever was happening in art. He never felt separate from that, and so being in Paris was a matter of coming to terms with the issues in contemporary art. To me, as I observed him at that time, that's one reason why he couldn't paint; there was too much to get together, and he had to get himself together from that distance. But Romie had dealt with that before. He had dealt with religious themes. You could find religious themes in a series of paintings that he did on Lorca. I have a painting at home where you have a grave-side lament for the *Death of a Bullfighter.*

Ailey: Did you guys have any political feelings in those days? Where were you? Were you definitely left of center, right of center, or in the middle?

Murray: You couldn't possibly be right of. . . . Well, I would think we were always radical, radically opposed, just to be what we were being—just to be articulate and to want to desegregate things and want to insert your two cents into the big dialogue was to be radical. You see, it wasn't any academic radicalism, it was a basic thing.

Ailey: Being black was radical in those days, just the fact of being a black man?

Murray: It was a sort of a regression that happened in the 60s when people went back and acted as if nothing had ever happened before. We couldn't do that, we were very much aware of James Weldon Johnson, W. E. B. Du Bois, Booker T. Washington, of Williams, of Carter Woodson, Benjamin Brawley; we were aware of that. It was already in the music of Ellington in the early 30s. He had written things like "Black Beauty," "Black and Tan Fantasy," all kinds of things. These things were simply a part of his sensibility.

Ailey: There's so much music in Romie's work. There's so much blues, spirituals; there's so much gospel; there's so much Mobile, Alabama: so much New Orleans, so much Mahalia Jackson. Where does Mobile come in? Romie, did you spend some time in Mobile?

Bearden: No, Charlotte, North Carolina. Jimmy is the only Northerner. On the other hand, he may be more Southern than all of us.

Ailey: What I want to know is, during the Depression did you always feel this connection to your roots? After the brown paper, what did you start to paint about? Did you stay with tempera? Did you start to paint with oils? When did you start the collage?

Bearden: Oh, that was way later. In 1941, Alvin, just before the outbreak of World War II, they had a big show and I was looking at the catalogue of all the painters who were painting out of their experiences; this changed later, but there was nothing else that you had to look forward to. You were there and this is what you did.

Alvin: I'm interested in the Depression, Romie. The WPA, you were there—there was support for artists. . . .

Bearden: The WPA was the greatest thing; that was paradoxical—here you were in the midst of the Depression—on 125th Street in the 30s and look who came out of there. There were the actors, writers, painters, all of the arts were given a chance to develop by the WPA.

Alvin: This is government subsidy on a very high level.

Bearden: Because there were practical people who did it, and they gave everybody a chance because, as Proust says, "You never know what direction talent may come."

Romare describes here the meaning of the first time he encountered Henri Matisse in Paris and, in a larger sense, how he was affected by the different social values embodied in the difference between French and American attitudes toward artists. Baldwin then speaks of the spiritual journey that the three of them experienced from the perspective of Paris.

Ailey: Romie, in those days were you aware of other painters? I mean, communication was not so easy in those days. Were you aware of Matisse, Picasso and others? Were you aware of African art? Were there conscious influences or were they all really governed out of the street?

Bearden: Oh yes, Alvin. I was sitting in a cafe in Paris and I think the French have a word. Jimmy, your French is more fluent than mine. Twilight, "le temps entre le chien et le loup," the time between the dog and the wolf, an old French expression. Someone hollered "La maitre passent," the master is passing by. I looked and here came Matisse, a young man supporting him and two young girls following. He may have been drawing them (as models) and they were taking him to a waiting car. All the waiters (about 10 or 12) ran to the curb and they began to applaud. Matisse was oblivious to this (Jimmy, they were passing the Dome) until the man pointed and said, "Master, this is for you." He was so delighted that he walked over and shook hands with all of the waiters. I was sitting back there as a young artist, and I was saying, "My God, this isn't Brigitte Bardot or Maurice Chevalier; you have a chance in Paris." Alvin, it meant so much to me. Just that one incident. They put poor Matisse in the car and they drove away. A few years after, he died. So you see, this was all around you in those days. I lived on the Rue Henri Barbusse, directly across from where Victor Hugo had written *Les Miserables;* Cesar Franson was nearby; Louis Pasteur's first laboratory was nearby. You were surrounded by these things. In the U.S., as great as it is, I don't know where Edgar Allan Poe lived; I know it's somewhere in the Bronx. But, all these things are torn down. Jimmy would know. Isn't this true, Jimmy? You were around all these things. They had plaques for all these things.

Baldwin: Oh, yes. You're right. It corroborated your right to your presence. It corroborated America. How can I put this? What we call the artistic endeavor. Essentially it is despised because it is not egalitarian. It is in this sense that what Al had to say about the South as distinguished from the Nouveau Renn and the whole advent of "Black Studies" in the 60s meant a great deal to me because in a sense—the details are very different—but to be born in Harlem as I was born, was to be born in a kind of vacuum. Whereas Al, who is much older than I am, was born where my father was born and grew up, in spite of everything else, was to be surrounded by—(and coming back to your point, Romie) surrounded by witnesses. Because the moment you described Matisse, the streets, the moment, the presence, really, of a certain kind of reality gives you the strength, a corroboration of something you already knew but you had to have the corroboration. Everybody has to have the corroboration. Everybody has to.

(I don't want to get in a discussion about America.) But, it is very important that you Romie, Al, all of us, we are speaking about a voyage which we all have to make seemingly far away to come full circle. To redeem a tradition which was not yet called a tradition because it was not yet written down except by Bessie Smith, Duke Ellington, and so forth, and by preachers like my father; and in the vacuum of Paris, in my case and your case, I began, I think, to understand my father's sermons and my own. This was a part of and not distinguished from and not an aberration of, not some weird kind of accident which happened to begin somewhere on the coast of West Africa and then became Jazz—New Orleans and then by some miracle became saved and became acceptable, etc., etc., etc., but an irreducible part of the human experience, the universal, the global experience as deep as that, as a turtle is that. It's impossible to describe the role of the church in this—it would take a long, long time to do that. It always struck me that out of that church which we, after all, in a way were forced to accept—one thing that black people did with it was to recognize all the symbols we were given—birth, resurrection, death—and take them completely out of the Christian context and take them back to where they began—the world which was called "pagan" or the world called "Africa," whatever you want to call the world before Europe.

Murray: The human context, the basic human concerns . . .

Baldwin: The basic necessity.

Murray: There's one thing I will pick you up on and then we'll go ahead, we'll orchestrate it; and that is literally, politically, historically, you could say they were forced but it didn't take much forcing because they were dealing with ritual, they were dealing with ceremony, and they were already disposed to that.

Baldwin: What I am saying is that we recognize something which in fact the white Christian had not been able to recognize.

Murray: Yes, well it had been extended or even attenuated, but immediately the Afro-American took it back to fundamentals.

Baldwin: That's what I am saying.

Here Al Murray expounds on the meaning of his usage of the word processing, and how it related to Baldwin and Bearden.

Ailey: Let's talk about Mobile.

Murray: What we're talking about, of course, is processing one's experience into art and I found, for my own purposes, the Renaissance creations—as important and indispensable as they were—were not adequate to the complexities I had to face. One of the things that drew me to Romie was that he was a man working in a medium that was different but working with the same experience, working out of a similar experience, out of the same tradition. He was trying to bring to bear all of the tools that were available, all the means of processing this. When I encountered Jimmy just the quality of the prose he was using meant that he was operating on another level of abstraction, so it was that sort of thing which moved our interest beyond just the study of what had been achieved during the Renaissance to what had been achieved in the world at large. I was concerned with the linguistic experiments of Joyce with the images and various things that were happening in poetry and fiction, but always with the thought of using them to process my own experience. You see, you don't have to go out with a flag about blackness or something like that. It was just a matter of how I processed my own experience. That's what I found out about Romie. If he was looking at Miró or somebody, it was how he would use the experience to deal with what he had to deal with.

Here Al Murray begins by relating how Ailey's choreography is a continuation of the same tradition of "processing" undertaken earlier by Bearden and Baldwin. Soon, the conversation moves on to individual comments on the emotional isolation they experienced in terms of their own identities as artists.

Bearden's early studies with George Grosz; his meeting with the great Spanish writer, Federico Garcia Lorca; and his paintings thematically derived from Lorca's *Death of a Bullfighter* are also dealt with in this section.

Murray: I would say that you yourself are the very embodiment of the process that we are talking about. You studied dance under Lester Horton, a very sophisticated exponent of modern dance, a pioneer, a man who was pushing back the language in terms of contemporary statement. He was avant garde, if there was such a thing. And yet, what you did with it immediately was to give to the anthology of dance, of choreography, *Revelations* and *Blues Suite.* In other words, you were processing experiences from Texas, Newport, or L.A. into fine art, and you did it by using the broadest possible language, and you were aware of what its relationship was to ballet or any other language of movement. This is the sort of thing that Romare was doing in Paris.

Ailey: What I want to know is how Romie started to deal with it during the Depression period, before Paris, and how you processed it. I know I took on the Graham influences, the Horton influences, the music, my own Texas experiences. I want to know how that devised itself in the work, Romie. How did Mobile, how did New Orleans get into your work? How did that all crystallize itself and get onto canvas?

Bearden: Not until later, Alvin.

Ailey: You didn't communicate that then?

Bearden: No, because at the time they thought that was not something for art. What you are talking about now . . .

Ailey: That experience that I was talking about?

Bearden: That Jimmy and Ralph Ellison and Al and the rest of them had to crystallize before it could get to you. Not to diminish you.

Ailey: Right, I understand.

Bearden: But I mean, that wasn't the thing then.

Ailey: But, you were processing this experience. . . .

Bearden: Yes, processing this experience. . . .

Ailey: Without societal acceptance, is that what you're telling me?

Bearden: Oh, completely so.

Baldwin: Without societal acceptance. Acceptance was a long way to go— without any societal possibility. No possibility at all. You were raised in a world where you learned this in school—you learned it from your teacher. You were very bewildered with the gap between your school and your house. And you were taught to despise yourself in school. Therefore, the idea of Romie Bearden being a painter, or Jimmy Baldwin or Alvin Ailey wasn't the world in which I grew up in any case—something unheard of; something there'd never been as far as I knew when I was growing up—anything resembling a black writer. One had to find that out by one's self.

Murray: Well, that's where ours was different; I [found out] because in Mobile you found that out, and we had that book of Negro American poetry that James Weldon Johnson edited around 1924 or 1925; all the poets, Langston Hughes, Countee Cullen, and among them was one Mobilian who was a graduate of Oberlin and whose name was Lucy Ariel Williams and her poem was called "Northbound" and it began something like this:

> The world ain't flat
> The world ain't round
> It's just one strip up and down
> North and South, South and North

And it went on in that way. We were so connected with the fact, I was so connected with the fact that you processed your own experiences into art and that you found the best way of doing it, the most comprehensive way or the way of getting as many of the nuances of it, because when you saw it fed back, it was too thin. But back to your question about Romie—Romie started out in a sort of classic—he has a sort of classic or basic natural history. It started out with political awareness and with political protest because he started out as a student of George Grosz, who was one of the great political satirists and an outstanding painter, too, at the Art Students League and whatnot. Then he wanted to deal with more of the complexities of his experience, and all that took more and more complicated equipment, so he became more involved with art. Tell them about your first paintings—the subject matter of the first paintings?

Bearden: You mean that I did on brown paper?

Murray: No, I mean the things that began to come together by the time of WPA and whatnot, or the time you were working on your themes.

Bearden: Oh, Lorca.

Murray: Yeah, Lorca.

Bearden: The *Death of the Bullfighter* because I had met Lorca.

Ailey: When he was here or that time in Europe?

Bearden: Here. Lorca was studying at Columbia, and he was very friendly with Langston Hughes, and he came with Langston Hughes, and this was before he went back to Spain. It meant nothing to me. I must admit that. I met him with Langston because Harlem was so small that when you gave a party everybody knew it and Lorca, Federico García Lorca, was a friend of Langston's and Langston squired him around Harlem, just like he did Mao Tse Tung.

Ailey: Mao Tse Tung was in this country?

Bearden: Oh, yes. He was studying here and was also a friend [of Langston's]. The only place he wanted to be was in Harlem and he was at Columbia too—Mao Tse Tung.

Murray: A lot of people acted like this never happened—they just don't take the time to look it up.

Ailey: They forget that Castro stayed at the Theresa, too, and that was the end of the Theresa.

Murray: But Lorca wrote a volume called *The Poet in New York* in which he does deal with Harlem.

Baldwin: Important Negroes, Negroes, Negroes. . . .

Ailey: But you reacted to it later, you painted later.

At this point, the four gentlemen discuss their early encounters with the traditions of black culture, in the days before formalized "Black Studies" existed.

That tradition is then discussed in the stylistic and thematic evolution of Romare's art, from the Lorca paintings to his most recent exhibit.

Connections are made, in this same context, to Ailey's ballets which, in effect, synthesize all forms of these traditions.

Finally, this tradition, this sense of cultural continuity, is seen as the basis for their approach to life and art.

Bearden: Later, later, Alvin, but I mean those people did meet. Just like Elmer Carter who was the editor of *Opportunity* used to go up and talk about someone called Harriet Tubman. It didn't mean anything to me until now, and he used to tell me stories because his father was a minister in Ossining and Harriet Tubman was a parishioner of his church. These things now come back to me. Just like Tanner, the painter, Henry O. Tanner. But they were always around us. These people were always accessible—not like Dr. Du Bois who everybody revered. He was hard to approach, but James Weldon

Johnson, if Jimmy was there, he could easily go up and talk to James Weldon Johnson, not to Dr. Du Bois, but all of them, Langston, of course, and Countee and Aaron Douglas, Jessie Fauset.

Murray: Jessie Fauset was teaching when Jimmy was in school.

Bearden: All of these people were around and a man named Dr. Seifert.

Ailey: Seifert?

Bearden: Seifert who had, he's dead now, his wife has as many books almost as Schomburg.

Murray: And Schomburg. . . .

Bearden: Yes, Schomburg had this great collection and so did Dr. Seifert. All of the young painters used to go to a brownstone on 138th Street and would go to his house. This was our first thing in black studies, so to speak, from Dr. Seifert; he wasn't really a doctor, he was a carpenter, but to us he was a doctor.

Murray: You also knew Alain Locke.

Bearden: Oh, Dr. Locke, he was a real doctor.

Murray: The intellectual, as it were, for the Renaissance. It was his book, *The New Negro,* which sort of made a permanent record of the Renaissance, which he did first as a guest editor for *Survey Graphic.*

Murray: On the Lorca theme, things that he [Bearden] is doing now are connected with what he did a long time ago. His most recent show, you have his whole profile, and before that you had *The Blues, Second Chorus of Blues,* those are two different shows; but Romie has long been interested in doing a series of paintings on a theme—*The Death of a Bullfighter,* and he did a number of paintings on that theme, so he was dealing with things. In the process of doing that he dealt with the religious element; he dealt with the sporting element; the ritualistic element; all these things were there.

Bearden: The things that you [Alvin] deal with in *Revelations.*

Ailey: Yes.

Murray: But you see, what is significant to me was that he was dealing with it by confronting a subject matter which was ostensibly not really his own; but he was pumping the authentic emotion from his own experience into it. Now he can deal with the subject matter, with the vernacular, idiomatic subject matter, and process it into a language of art.

Bearden: So we have a definite tradition, a definite tradition which we four are a part of.

Murray: And whatever you address yourself to. You see, you don't always have to deal with the idiomatic in order to make use of (let's call it) feelings, which is essentially idiomatic. You know what I mean.

Bearden: And then Alvin came.

Alvin: And the Company, right.

Bearden: And he just tore it up.

Alvin: Continuing the tradition. 1950 being reborn in 1974.

Murray: It's about crystallization, elaboration and refinement of the basic things; keeping the human content intact, the basic values in terms of which one lives. Kenneth Burke used the term "equipment for living," that is a way of encompassing experience, a way of coming to terms with experience. Whether one does it with words, does it with movements, or does it with images, it is basic equipment for living. It's not just "oo-la-la."

Baldwin: And also all of these arbitrarily called "art forms," they are all connected, because we all need each other, we learn from each other—the way Alvin choreographed the dance or the movement in Romie.

Alvin: The rhythm in Romie's work, the coloring, the form and the texture and the use of space and the dynamics and all of those things, it's the same.

Baldwin: Yes, exactly—it's the same thing.

Bearden: It's the same as in your prose. The difference in Alvin, where he has it over myself and you [Baldwin] and Albert is that his form combines all of it. You have the dance, the art, music, writer, you've got it all over us.

Alvin: And it's there living and breathing in front of you. And the long legs and the beautiful feet.

Bearden: You've got it all combined in one. Don't you feel jealous? I feel jealous of you.

Alvin: No, no, I don't feel jealous; I feel supported; I feel like I am a part of a tradition that will long continue, and I am very proud.

Bearden: We're all going to do great librettos for you.

Alvin: Yes, I hope so.

Murray: The real arrogance and the real progressiveness of the artist is that, underneath, he really wants to prevail. He wants his image to take over.

Baldwin: He wants to change his image.

Murray: I would like for people to think of how it was in terms of schooling, in terms of Buster Brown and you think you have your methods; you have your metaphors. Romie has his images on the wall or his tensions on the wall even if they are abstract. This mirrored reality for Americans, and contemporary man at large could see himself in terms of these images—these renderings of experiences—and come away from what we have tried to do with a little more refined equipment for the complex situations that we now face as contemporary men.

Baldwin: For life.

Murray: If it's enduring—the experiments exist only for the purpose of enduring and it's not a matter of changing all the time, it's a matter of getting something that will last and Alvin has that. He can't get away from *Revelations* because it's perennial; it continues to grow and people ask for it. He might have any number of new things, but they call for that and that is a proper response to an artistic achievement and that's the way Romie's newest paintings connect with his oldest paintings—the themes—and people are now writing about the fact that he deals with themes, but that was there from the very beginning. Now he can get more English on the ball; now he can get more instruments up and get more dancers on the stage.

This final excerpt begins with a discussion of the artist Beauford Delaney, and how much his life and work revealed to all of them. It concludes with a touching affirmation of just how much Bearden the man, and Bearden the artist, means to the others, and, really, to all of us.

Ailey: Beauford Delaney was a very important figure to you guys in the 50s, in the 60s, in the 70s . . . a giant of a man who also found himself in Paris.

Baldwin: Well the truth about that is, in a way, if I hadn't known Beauford, I might never have known Romie or been able to see Romie's work, that is to say his journey. I met Beauford when I was a high school kid. Beauford was the only, then, black artist, living black artist that I could put my hands out and touch. He was a painter. I trusted him, I loved him and I used to watch Beauford look at something, and for a long time I didn't know, I would just literally watch his eyes and try to see what he looked at. I followed him around like a school boy, in fact, which is what I was. I watched his canvasses and I began to see, but I couldn't express it that way; something which I'd never, never seen before in this frail, short black man who was already a kind of patriarch. His studio was already a kind of haven for many, many people, all kinds of people. Beauford came to Paris five years after I did and shortly after, you and I met and he knew who you [Bearden] were much better than I did. I knew Jacob Lawrence a little bit and I'd been involved essentially in language or rhetoric or in music, in a way, because I think the whole root is somewhere in the music. I began to hear that in Beauford's canvasses, and I began to see it in your very different journey. It's very difficult to express that; it's a curious process, to use Al's word, which carries you both back, simultaneously back and forward in time. This is to say you lean, yet you're empowered finally by someone else's testimony; to reach back and claim what has always been yours; yet with that same gesture, you're empowered to move forward. So, the chain, in effect, is never broken. You see what I mean?

Bearden: Yes.

Baldwin: And that is what, that's all I can say about, for example, you. It was an extraordinary thing to me in 1950 until this hour, from the first things I saw of yours until the last show I saw of yours. In a sense I begin to see things that you have not yet begun. Does that make sense to you?

Bearden: Right.

Baldwin: It's a tremendous affirmation.

Bearden: Do you remember one day, Alvin, Richard Long, and myself were waiting for you [Baldwin] because we knew Beauford meant so much to you and Beauford was lost?

Baldwin: Ah yes.

Bearden: And we'd been to the embassy, we'd been to the police, and no one knew where Beauford was, and we were waiting for you because Beauford meant so much to Jimmy. He lived on this small street . . .

Baldwin: He lived on Rue Vercingetorix.

Bearden: Vincengeteroix.

Baldwin: Yeah, 53.

Bearden: Ah, the name of the old man who fought the Romans, the Goths or something.

Baldwin: That's right.

Bearden: You know how old that place was and there was Beauford. He said to me, there were a group of people, Jimmy; one day he said, (somebody talked about old,) he said, "No one is ever old or young, life is so short." No one, Alvin, is ever old or young.

Alvin: Or young.

Bearden: And people loved Beauford. He was such a wonderful artist; he was such a wonderful man.

Alvin: The way we love you.

Murray: That meant so much to Jimmy.

Bearden: Well, I mean Beauford even more so.

Baldwin: Well, no, no—one cannot put it that way. It's not a more or less so, it's tremendous . . . tremendous processing, again to use Al's word.

Bearden: Just wonderful.

Baldwin: Which we all finally need.

The Book, Like the Man, Is Deliberately Reserved

Robert C. Trussell / 1986

From *The Kansas City Star,* February 9, 1986, pp. 1L, 7L. Reprinted with permission by *The Kansas City Star.*

For Albert Murray, committing Count Basie's autobiography to paper was a little like stomping the blues.

"It was just like playing music, just like we were sitting at the piano," Mr. Murray said in a telephone interview from New York. "So the composition was a real collaboration. He knew how to work with arrangers, so I was an arranger."

In 1977, the late Willard Alexander, a theatrical booking agent who had handled the Count Basie Orchestra for many years, approached Mr. Murray about helping the legendary bandleader write his autobiography. The work began in earnest in 1978 and reached fruition with the publication Jan. 31 of the 400-page *Good Morning Blues.*

Mr. Murray is scheduled to be in Kansas City on Monday to promote the book.

History buffs with a fondness for vivid accounts of the lurid days of the Pendergast machine in Kansas City may find the book more interesting for what it omits than for what it includes.

But Mr. Murray, 69, said the diplomatic sidestepping and outright exclusion of details that might have proved embarrassing for Mr. Basie and others—and fascinating for general readers—were a direct expression of the Count's overriding sense of propriety.

As an example, Mr. Murray cited the legendary taped-recorded interviews he conducted with Mr. Basie.

"I had a little clip-on mike, and he would forget about the mike until he got into something that would be embarrassing to somebody else, and then he would turn the mike off and say, 'Now let me tell you about it.' . . . That's why the book is so true to him. It's so true to his personality. He never let it all hang out, because that was not the true Count Basie."

Even so, Mr. Murray said, Mr. Basie had no problem with others who may

46

have chosen to paint a more descriptive and detailed portrait of his life and times.

"Count would say, "That's OK, as long as it's true, but I don't want it in my book.'

"The omissions were intentional. He had no intention of going on record about anything he had seen or heard about the workings of the Pendergast machine . . . Once he became a public figure, he never wanted to get involved in public controversies. He was always aware of the damage a careless word could do to others' reputations. That's the sense of propriety he had."

Nevertheless, the book is full of allusions to the less refined aspects of Kansas City's days as a "wide-open" town, and it is forthright in its numerous references to the prevalence of alcohol.

Mr. Murray, an author of fiction and journalism whose books include the award-winning *Stomping the Blues,* said the musicians of the 1920s and '30s were participants in a bacchanalian celebration of sorts and that a certain amount of overindulgence went with the territory.

"This is a music of celebration," Mr. Murray said. "It's good-time music. They played the blues, but they do what I said in my other book: They stomp the blues away. It's a celebration of life itself, and they celebrate a fertility ritual . . . We're dealing with the fundamentals of life.

"He said, 'I want to go out on the road and do this,' and in the process he became an artist. But he never had to divorce that in his mind from the world of entertainment."

Food, drink and other hedonistic pursuits were a part of the fabric of life, and some of those who were part of the scene paid a dear price. Others, such as Mr. Basie, survived to an advanced age and left a spectacular body of work.

"It was not detrimental to Basie," Mr. Murray said. "He was in striking distance of his 80th birthday. A lot of them burned out in their 20s, but Basie was just getting started at that time."

Mr. Murray said he tried to capture Mr. Basie's conversational tone. The effect is a little like sitting down with the Count to listen to stories about the good old days.

After considering Mr. Basie's life and career, Mr. Murray decided that a good place to begin the story was in the late '20s, when Mr. Basie encountered the Blue Devils, the Oklahoma City band that would have a lifelong influence on his music.

"We decided to go right on through the Blue Devils experience just like he remembered it. You could shoot it right from the book, you could shoot it like a script."

In many cases, Mr. Murray said, Mr. Basie's recollection of specific dates was a little fuzzy, and so the author sought verification in the microfilm files of several black newspapers, including the *Chicago Defender,* the *Oklahoma City Black Dispatch* and *The Kansas City Call.*

Mr. Murray accompanied Mr. Basie on a visit to Kansas City in the late '70s, and the Count showed him many of the historic sites in the 18th and Vine street area.

If Mr. Basie emerges as a man with few, if any, political instincts, Mr. Murray said that was the way he was. Indeed, the Count was an artist who performed music for the sake of music, whose success and dignity made an eloquent political statement.

"The political overtones of the book are inescapable because they're so affirmative," Mr. Murray said. "Here's a man who was most fortunate because he never had to think about retiring. You notice, nowhere in that book does he go out and get another job. He was only interested in music. And when he had a lot of money—and he made a lot of money—he couldn't stand to be down in the Bahamas too long. After two or three days, he wanted to be back out playing and having a good time.

"We're talking about a success story of a person who was not trying to be successful in order to be rich. With Basie, the pressure of money meant being able to hire guys and pay them. This time we're living in now, so many people are worried about how many gold and platinum records they have— but they didn't care."

A Jazz Jam with a Pen

Joe Cohen / 1986

From *The West Side Spirit,* through March 3, 1986, pp. 13, 14. Reprinted by permission of *The West Side Spirit.*

1. Vamp Till Ready

When Count Basie, that metronomic master of sophisticated swing, decided to embark upon the autobiographical adventure in 1978, he asked Willard Alexander, a longtime business associate, to help him find a co-writer. Alexander began by asking Alec Wilder, the songwriter and scholar of American popular swing, who immediately recommended the man who was undoubtedly the best equipped to orchestrate the memoirs of Count Basie—West Side novelist and essayist Albert Murray.

"He wondered what type of story his life would add up to," Murray says of his first meeting with Basie. "I made a suggestion about where we would start and how it would go, and he thought it was a great idea. So I made a working outline, and from then on it was a collaboration, just like when you work with an arranger."

Murray and Basie devised a story line that would begin with a pivotal moment in the bandleader's life—the first time he heard the Oklahoma City band known as the Blue Devils—and then move through flashbacks from Basie's birth in Red Bank, New Jersey, right up to 1984.

"But the piano intro," Murray says, "is Basie on the train roaring from London to Liverpool, when he decides to tell his story. It's in italics, just like Basie: he would play those italicized piano intros. But it doesn't necessarily go to the first chorus, it might go to the out chorus . . ."

Murray interrupted his own work—the second installment of a fiction trilogy that began with 1974's *Train Whistle Guitar*—to work with Basie. When the Count died in 1984, the book had reached its first draft. It appeared last month as *Good Morning Blues.*

2. First Chorus

Albert Murray lives with his wife, Mozelle, in an apartment on West 132 Street in Harlem. The few walls not covered with books are covered with paintings and prints, mostly by Romare Bearden, in whose art Murray has

49

found "the visual equivalent of the blues." Murray's art, like Bearden's, partakes of the same pleasure, irony, class, sophistication, and, to use one of Murray's favorite words, *stylization* found in the cultural expression known as jazz.

Murray's analysis of blues and jazz music, revealed in his books *The Omni-Americans* and *Stomping the Blues,* was a new riff for anthropologists and cultural critics. The blues may be sad and weary, Murray told us, but blues *music* is not; it's a complex, positive and self-aware art form that pulls one out of individual sadness and into group affirmation. Thus the blues artist is not a martyr. He's a hero.

"You proceed from primordial ritual," Murray says, "that is the basic re-enactment of a survival technique. If you do it in just a flat ceremonial manner it's called ritual. If you do it supervised by a priesthood it's called religion. If you give it its ultimate playful extension, elaboration and refinement, then it's art. It's got everything in it. Basie represented that refinement, the refinement of the fundamentals of the idiom. That is, *swing.*"

3. Riff

Murray speaks of *Good Morning Blues* in terms of theme and riff, composition and chorus. As a writer, he's got riffs of his own: the color blue, the blue of guitar strings and bayou moans, the warm, glowing blue of the Saturday Night Function, the swinging blue of the Blue Devils. And trains: the lonesome whistle of the Number Four (with the bluesman's guitar clanging the bell) and the clickety-clack syncopation of the wheels. You can hear these riffs in *Train Whistle Guitar,* in *Stomping the Blues,* and, if any more proof is needed, in Count Basie's voice in *Good Morning Blues.*

"Duke Ellington," Murray recalls of another friend, "was unusual in that his mind was anthropological enough to know that he was operating on the level of railroad onomatopoeia when he was playing jazz. The drums would become the locomotive pistons, and you're playing the whistle up there. Now B. B. King couldn't tell you that in a million years. He's made a whole life and a million dollars *doing* it, but he can't *tell* you that . . . you don't get that insight from him. You get the goosepimples that come from the sound of his music!"

But musicians, Murray says, don't need to have the ability to analyze the context and meaning of their music. That's for writers to do.

4. Second Chorus

Chuckling that "if you're going to be a big-league writer you have to do a lot of work," Murray pulls out a box of xeroxed newspaper clippings and magazine articles, all classified by year. Murray did the research, tracing the obscure burlesque show that brought Basie to the midwest, mapping the itinerary of the bands Basie played with. Then he would read the clips to the Count, who would jump in and solo with his more specific recollections.

"I'd evoke it for him," Murray explains. "I'd play the piano for him." He gestures to the clippings. "These are the notes that I was playing on the piano."

Basie, according to Murray, didn't trust reporters, and rarely opened up to writers. "Did you ever try to interview Basie? Most people figured, 'Count Basie's book is coming? It'll be like this . . .' "

He holds up his thumb and forefinger. A very thin book.

Good Morning Blues runs 400 pages. It may not be total recall, but it's a very scenic train ride.

Jazz Rules Life of Basie Biographer

Robert Becker / 1987

From *The Daily Progress* (Charlottesville, Virginia), March 19, 1987, pp. D1, D3. Reprinted by permission of *The Daily Progress*.

The man that jazz legend Duke Ellington called the "unsquarest man I know" sits beneath a stern portrait of James Madison in the Colonnade Club at the University of Virginia and improvises about music, life and art in a way that both the Duke and another jazz legend, Count Basie—and even the former president—would have applauded.

"What resembles a jazz arrangement more that the Constitution?" asks Albert Murray, novelist and "arranger" of the acclaimed autobiography of Basie, *Good Morning Blues.* "Jazz is a metaphor for our entire society."

Jazz helps to explain the working of Murray's eclectic mind. Hours before he is to deliver the UVa English department's Peter Rushton Lecture on this Wednesday, Murray's train of thought boogies from talk of Joyce, Johnny Hodges and Greek drama to bebop, classical architecture and Kansas City blues.

He talks about Faulkner and Hemingway with the same authority that he discusses the Blue Devils or Sarah Vaughan. He nervously thrashes his compact frame on the couch, lurching closer to his listener and punctuating his explanations with "You see what I mean?"

Jazz is the common thread that unifies his thinking. You have to have a mind as quick as Duke Ellington's fingers to follow the riffs and breaks that Murray throws at you.

"That's what jazz is all about," says the 71-year-old Murray in his low, raspy voice. "Change and creativity. You're operating on the frontier all the time."

The seven years Murray spent collaborating with Basie on the autobiography were just a long jam session. Murray, a writer, professor and musician himself, employed Basie's penchant for rehearsal to fashion a book described as "one of the most finished and evocative life histories of an American musician ever written."

"Just like he never got tired of playing a song over and over again, he didn't get tired of my asking questions about the past," said Murray, who

often traveled with Basie, interviewing him after rehearsals or before per-
formances. "He'd tell me something, I'd get the dates, and we'd gradually
fill in the details.

"He was a dream to work with."

Murray, however, never dreamed he would be involved in such a project.
Growing up in Mobile, Ala., he saw himself involved in less scholarly pursuits.

"I thought that I'd major in physical education or something like that," he
says. "But then I started seeing all those 38-year-old coaches, and realized it
wasn't for me."

Murray studied English literature at Tuskegee Institute and was active in
drama. He wrote plays and acted in local little theater productions but was
never interested in music.

"I was too interested in literature," he says. "I translated Latin and read
everything I could get my hands on."

Not surprisingly, Murray chose teaching as his profession. He studied at
New York, Chicago, and Michigan universities, and has taught at Colgate,
Columbia, and Emory. He was also an officer in the Air Force for 20 years.

"It took me a while to discover my own aesthetic," he said. "You know,
that figure in the carpet that Henry James talks about."

The figure in the carpet, that shadowy intellectual superstructure that informs all of his work, turns out to be a funky combination of German author
Thomas Mann's philosophy and Kansas City blues. Jazz, says Murray, per-
meates our literature and culture.

Such a view is to be expected from a man who uses jazz to teach Sophocles' *Oedipus.*

"Look at any jazz piece," he said, "You've got the structure of a Greek
play right there."

Murray holds his hands out and plays an imaginary piano, imitating the
Basie style of cool control, directing the blending of horns and percussion
with piano. He closes his eyes, tilts his head and smiles. The vibrancy of
Basie and his music has not lessened since the Count's death in 1984.

"You can deal with jazz just as music, as the specific idiom of Afro-American expression," Murray says still smiling. "But if you bring enough to it,
you're dealing with life. And that's what makes it universal."

Talking with Albert Murray:
A Hero and the Blues

Gene Seymour / 1991

From *New York Newsday,* November 24, 1991, Fanfare section, pp. 34–35. Newsday, Inc., Copyright 1991. Reprinted with permission.

What the madeleine was for Marcel Proust, the opening of Jelly Roll Morton's "Kansas City Stomp" is for Albert Murray. Once that *ba-doo-badoo-ba-doo-badoo-ba-doo-badoo-ba-doo-badoo-bap—MOP!* fanfare reaches Murray's ears, the past, with all of its smells, sights and sounds, opens its arms and embraces the rest of his senses.

Music like this can transport Murray from his book-lined apartment just off Lenox Avenue in Harlem into a chinaberry-scented world of dirt roads, boyhood dreams, mother-wit, backwoods legends and communal love that somehow got left out of all the grim case studies of growing up poor and black in the Deep South.

Not that violence or hardship or racism are absent from Murray's memory bank. In fact, one of the key scenes in *The Spyglass Tree* (Pantheon, $20), Murray's new novel and the second in a planned trilogy of semi-autobiographical fiction about a young black man's coming of age in Alabama of the 1920s and '30s, involves the vicious beating of a black man by a prominent white man near Tuskegee Institute—which Murray attended in the mid-'30s.

But since Murray has spent the balance of his adult life throwing glitches into narrow sociological views of African-American life, the beating isn't depicted in a manner that demands the reader's pity. Rather, it is shown as part of the bending, twisting, undulating flow of life in those not-so-distant days—which, as Murray shows in both the new novel and its predecessor, *Train Whistle Guitar* (1974), had a commensurate share of good times as well.

The response by the black townspeople to the beating is likewise depicted in unsentimental, tough-minded fashion befitting descendants of slaves, who, as Murray has written elsewhere, were the first true American existentialists. "Every day, the black slave woke up seeing that nothing much was good and then decided not to commit suicide." See Camus nod.

This implacable and affirmative resolve to transcend hardship gave life to the blues, which are the foundation of African-American music—and, arguably, of the nation's soul. Certainly the blues are the core of Murray's aesthetics. In such books as *The Omni-Americans* (1970), *The Hero and the Blues* (1973) and *Stomping the Blues* (1976), he has honed a prose style that carries the tender, lyrical and big-beat cadences of down-home swing. You have to use your ears as much as your eyes to read him.

The components of this style—and, for that matter, of Murray's nimble, colorful patter—are as varied as the ingredients of the richest, thickest, tastiest gumbo you ever had. Murray has drawn inspiration from every jazz musician he's heard—especially his hero, friend and patron Duke Ellington. And another old friend, Romare Bearden, the late, great African-American master of the epic collage, maintains an active influence on Murray's muse. Original work by Bearden adorns the walls of Murray's apartment.

The books on his desk—*The Blue Fairy Book, Remembrance of Things Past* and editions of James Joyce's *Ulysses* and *Finnegans Wake*—suggest the mix of inspiration he's after in his own elegiac fiction. One finds throughout his work references to André Malraux and Thomas Mann. Then there's the considerable influence of William Faulkner (first editions of whose work are prominently displayed on his shelves). In fact, Murray's recently republished *South to a Very Old Place* (1972) may well be the only existing model for Faulknerian literary criticism / reportage / autobiography.

"From Faulkner, I got the challenge of dealing with time," Murray says. "But the *economy* I got from Hemingway. See, he was the master of the epoch-making style. That's a style so natural that it doesn't seem to be a style. You know, people talk about who they like and don't like [to read]. They like Henry James. They like E. M. Forster. They like Anthony Powell. But when they edit it and they want to get the paragraphs right and they want the readers to see the sweat on the wine bottle, they'll put on Hemingway's glasses to see better.

"It's like they talk about that macho stuff, but . . . well, let me show ya something." And he hops from his chair, faster than any 75-year-old man should be capable of, grabs off the shelf a copy of Hemingway's *Winner Take Nothing* and reads the frontpiece: *"Unlike all other forms of lutte or combat, the conditions are that the winner shall take nothing, neither his ease nor his pleasure, not any notions of glory; nor if he win far enough shall there by any reward within himself."*

Murray snaps the book shut, "Now *that there* is the human condition! *'La*

Condition Humaine,' as Malraux called it . . . Recognizing that this is our shared destiny should make possible the virtues of charity, of mercy." He laughs. "You know, when you're 75, this is how you think all the time."

Actually, Murray's been thinking such things for a long time. He believes that they lie at the core of all great art, whether the artist in question is Pablo Picasso or Sidney Bechet. He has also tried to bring such aesthetic considerations into the great race relations discourse—which, he believes, too often yields the floor to sociologists and polemicists who ignore or dismiss the complexities that he has worked to dramatize.

And yet, whenever people like Murray have suggested that there's a different way of viewing the black experience than what doctrinaire nationalists and firebrands promote, they have been viewed as being "not black enough." Of this phenomenon, Murray says, "I think it, well . . . there's a big problem of . . . whadya call it? . . . *mode.* We got stuck at a certain phase of this insurgence or rebellion or movement where taking a militant stance was the thing to do. Jimmy Baldwin being sassy to white folks . . . Hey, that's a good gig. White folks *love* being cussed out and told, 'You've done this to me, you've done that.' Because you've defined yourself to them as a victim.

"My response? I think of Duke and how people couldn't understand why he was smiling all the time and why he wasn't militant enough. And Duke would say to me, 'Man, I'm not gonna let a bunch of second-rate people like that impress me. My momma told me I was blessed. I'm gonna listen to *them?*' " This story summons a laugh from Murray that's so loud it almost overcomes the sound of a siren screaming outside his apartment building.

An Interview with Albert Murray, Author of *The Spyglass Tree*

John Seigenthaler / 1992

From a tape of a conversation for the television series "A Word on Words," produced by WDCN, a member of the Southern Educational Communications Association of public television stations. The interview took place on October 9, 1992, in the studios of WDCN in Nashville, Tennessee. John Seigenthaler, former chair of the Freedom Forum First Amendment Center at Vanderbilt University and Publisher Emeritus of Nashville's daily paper *The Tennessean,* hosted this segment of the series, which was first broadcast on February 2, 1993. Roberta Maguire transcribed and edited the interview, which is printed here by permission of the Nashville Public Television Council, Inc., and John Seigenthaler.

JS: Good evening, ladies and gentlemen, and once again welcome to "A Word on Words." This evening our guest is in my judgment one of the finest writers in this country—not just in my judgment; many critics have said so. Albert Murray, welcome to "A Word on Words."

AM: It's nice to be here.

JS: It's nice to have you. It's nice to have you particularly to talk about Scooter. *The Spyglass Tree,* which is the book here, and that's the paperback edition just out, is really the sequel to your earlier book *Train Whistle Guitar.* In *Train Whistle Guitar* you created seventeen, eighteen years ago, this little boy Scooter, and now you've brought him to young adulthood; you have put him in a college, unnamed, and once more you enmesh us in the life and times of Scooter. And I have to ask you what I know you've been asked again and again and again, how much of Scooter is Albert Murray?

AM: Well, a lot of him is Albert Murray. The way he feels and his outlook on life represent either my own outlooks or my aspirations, but you handle these things in a literary fashion. The whole idea of literature is to stylize the raw experience of your everyday life into aesthetic statement. In order to do that you're really trying to make a story. It has to have a certain design. Just as a painting has to have a design, so does a narrative have to have a design. You have the freedom, then, of doing all kinds of things. You can give some of your characteristics to other characters, other people in the book; you can

57

appropriate some of their ideals and characteristics and their skills and so forth to yourself. But overall you want to make a statement. So in a sense Scooter represents a lot of Albert Murray, but a lot of other people in those books represent a lot of Albert Murray.

JS: Well, I'm sure that's right. It would be close to correct to suggest that Scooter's fictional town of Gasoline Point is somewhere near Nokomis, Alabama.

AM: It's really Magazine Point, on the outskirts of Mobile just where the Chickasabogue Creek comes off of Mobile River and goes on up and across the canebrakes. And it was a "magazine point" back during the Civil War. But by the time that Scooter came along in the 1920s it was a storage yard for the Gulf Refining Company; so it became a gasoline point.

JS: It was an easy transition—and is it fair to say that the unnamed university in which Scooter enrolled as one of the "talented tenth" is Tuskegee?

AM: Yes, it's based on Tuskegee. You know, if you sit for a portrait for Picasso or somebody else you might have two ears on this side, but it's still your portrait. So you can make distortions or abstractions or you can stretch the design this way or that. You know from my other books that I think that sociology adds up to an inadequate image and that I don't want to be confused with a case history, so with Scooter and his environs we're dealing in metaphor. I don't mind using something as a point of departure, but if you turn around and nail it down to that, then it takes away the dimension which I'm trying to describe.

JS: I guess it takes away the hard core reality of life if you try to superimpose a sociological moral or sociological answer. I think you've escaped that in all the books you've written.

AM: Well, that's what I've been trying to do. You have to have deliberate distortion. The monument I describe in my book obviously is not the Booker Washington monument on the campus, yet some of the other buildings I describe are exactly in place.

JS: Now let me ask you about people around Scooter. I take it that you feel that fiction gives you the opportunity to tell a story that is much broader than "a life," and that biography would really be restrictive and would be too factual and might give the dimension of a sociological study: my life and the lessons I have learned. You don't have to worry about that, the fact of that, in fiction. But you've only done two works of fiction. Is that accurate?

AM: Right.

JS: Well, seventeen years between *Train Whistle Guitar* and *The Spyglass Tree,* that's just about the period of time it took Scooter to get from Gasoline Point to Tuskegee.

AM: [Laughs.] That's right.

JS: And I was wondering, are we going to wait seventeen more years before we hear from the trilogy?

AM: Definitely not. I hope that you can see it next year. But there were other things happening in the meantime. When I finished *Train Whistle Guitar,* I was ready to go into what became *The Spyglass Tree,* but my editor, knowing that throughout my work I deal with what I call the blues idiom—jazz and so forth, the content as well as the form, structure, and procedure—encouraged me to write *Stomping the Blues,* and that became widely distributed and discussed, and that led to Count Basie to ask me to help him—

JS: With his own story—

AM: Right. So that gave me a chance to look at somebody else's life—the whole thing, boyhood and all—with the sense of story that I was already into. And he could respond to that because he knew that he wanted his life, the facts of his life, stylized into a narrative. He knew that it had to be a stylization. You're taking the secular and moving it into the profane—or rather taking the profane and moving it into the sacred. You see what I mean?

JS: I do.

AM: And you're taking it out of its ordinary nuts and bolts and you're making a statement out of it. And he could understand that.

JS: Now the life Scooter lived, I think it's probably characteristic of millions of lives of millions of black youngsters born into a south that was unfriendly territory to them—they knew it was a hostile world. You write of the isolated black community inside the larger community with some feeling, and I think maybe through Scooter I had a sense for the first time of a culture that in some ways still exists—that those little southern black communities, even though some now exist not in rural settings or on the outskirts of major cities, but as part of an inner city, that some of that same culture is still there.

AM: But the other thing, see, even more important than that is trying to make Scooter universal; you deal as accurately as possible with the idiomatic particulars, but you're trying to get the universal implications. And, just as I wanted, the first fan letters I got were from white southern boys—maybe because they read more widely and so forth, but that's what I wanted: I wanted everybody to be Scooter just as I was Ulysses, just as I was Seigfried, or Beowulf, or Roland—they'll want to be Scooter. Anytime a guy picks up a horn, a trumpet, and puts it in his mouth, he wants to be Louis Armstrong. Anytime he goes to a mike and wants to sing a love song to a girl, he wants to be Louis Armstrong. If he gets a band in front of him, he wants to be Duke Ellington. He may look like a Viking or he may look like a Teuton, but he wants to be Duke Ellington. That's what I want him to be as an American.

JS: It's interesting that you say that, because the next thing I was going to say to you is that not too long ago sitting in that chair was an author named Ferroll Sams who has just completed a trilogy of his own white counterpart of Scooter, and the experiences are phenomenally similar. I wish that I could get you and Ferroll Sams together.

AM: [Laughs.] Let's work it out.

JS: Because I think that he has created a whole widespread audience just built around this one child.

AM: Well, one of the most pleasant things about the reviews of both these books, you see, is that one of them talks about me and Mark Twain, not necessarily in terms of the quality—

JS: Oh, I think it is the quality—I'll tell you I don't agree with that.

AM: Well, the critics talk about Stephen Dedalus, and they talk about Wilhelm Meister, but they should also have talked about [Thomas Mann's] Joseph because I've already spelled that out in *Hero and the Blues.* Joseph is my boy—he's a golden brown hero who goes into a country in bondage and turns out to be the savior of the country. That is the mission of any epic hero, and I've seen any number of things that have happened during this last generation where there are brownskin heroes who want to be the savior of the country. In that sense, so as to get beyond the sociological categories and into the epical categories, I want him to be epical so that anybody can identify with him. So it has all these dimensions, and at the same time you're trying to get those idiomatic particulars as accurate as possible: you want to beat everybody with the local color. You want your local color to be as believable as Hemingway's local color—or Faulkner's. You can't get by Faulkner. You've got to come through Faulkner. You've got to do something so that if you're in a jam session with Faulkner he would say, "Hey, that was a good solo."

JS: Well, you put down the comparison with Twain, but many critics have said Scooter and Huckleberry Finn are cut from the same cloth. Many other critics look at your body of fiction—and it's still evolving—and because of that local color, and I think because of the cadence and flavor of your writing, have compared you with Faulkner. I mean I don't think that is an exaggerated analogy at all.

AM: No, but that helps the statement—

JS: Must be good for your ego. But I'm amazed at the way you present it in that self-effacing manner, Albert—

AM: One has ambitions—you see what I mean? It's like Jack Johnson from Port Arthur, Texas, set out to be the world's heavyweight champion boxer, and went all the way to Sydney, Australia, to do so. It's that type of thing. I don't want people to lose sight of that. I'm trying to be the title of my first book—the Omni-American. I want to create a character that all Americans would like to be like, that all contemporary people would like to be like. And with Armstrong and Ellington feeding in there with Faulkner and Hemingway and Twain and Thomas Mann and André Malraux and Goethe and all these people—we ought to be able to do that at this time in the United States. We should develop a sensibility which encompasses what the experience of man is at this stage of the game in the twentieth century— the quintessential twentieth century man—and that's the type of ambition that goes into that. And you do it by looking right at that little postage stamp of a world that Faulkner talks about and trying to do the best you can.

JS: I'm interested in what prompts you from time to time to take on a subject. Blues obviously has been a part of the core of your life—the music itself. The scene that sums it up best I guess is in *The Spyglass Tree* in which you talk about Scooter's encounter with a woman, an attractive woman who has all these records, and—

AM: Hortense Hightower.

JS: Hortense Hightower. And they spend this time together; literally time runs out for Scooter. He has to go back to the campus. But then you did *South to a Very Old Place*. It's a natural theme, but I'm interested in the timing. I mentioned seventeen years between the first two books of the Scooter trilogy, of which the third is going to come soon. How did *South to a Very Old Place* come to be? What prompted you to write it at the time you wrote it?

AM: *South to a Very Old Place*? That's a very easy question. We were just talking off camera about Willie Morris. Well, Willie Morris was the editor of *Harper's*. He initiated a series called "Going Home in America." And then he wrote a book himself, which was called *North Toward Home.* So he decided that I should be one of the authors to contribute to that series. Somebody went to the midwest, somebody went to this place, somebody went to that place—I decided to go downhome. I concocted this title and old Willie liked it so much that he said, "I want to buy the title." So having decided to go south and deal with certain things, I soon found the project had gotten beyond the article; it became a book. I tried to write a nonfiction novel to the extent that it would not be a report but it would be a metaphor—in the narrative form. You would have flashbacks, you would have everything that a novel would have, but it wouldn't be geared to a specific time as a report, although it would contain the essence of a report of a journey. I saw it as an epilogue in the sense that it could function as an epilogue to this trilogy, before it was done.

JS: If I tell my son to read Albert Murray, I should tell him to read the trilogy, Scooter from one, two, three, and then follow those books with *South to a Very Old Place*?

AM: It really wouldn't matter that much, but if you read it afterwards, you can see him looking back. But speaking of time, there's a sequence in the current manuscript I'm writing in which Scooter goes to see some guy up on Sugar Hill in Harlem and this guy's a retired tap dancer named Royal Highness. And he's got all kinds of tales to tell him and so forth and he tells him, "Yeah, young soldier, come on in here and let me tell you about so and so." He talks to him like that—

JS: Scooter by this time has been in the army, is in the army, I take it—

AM: Well, now the army experience doesn't come in. That's why you can't follow it too closely—

JS: When he says, "Come in, young soldier—"

AM: No, he means young soldier in the idiomatic—the barbershop—sense of the word. "You're the troops," you know, "I want to see what you splibs are doing about them jaspers down there, twisting all those dials" and so forth. "Come out, young soldier," that type of thing. When I wrote that stuff, I was in Hollywood sometime then—I must have been in my forties—so I visualized him as being maybe in his late fifties or sixties and retired. When

I came back to deal with him—and he's now set—I was seventysome years old. [Laughs.] I realized I had created a very good old man—something of a curmudgeon, but you know with so much achievement and so much good will that he's not really a curmudgeon. But I was actually older than old Royal Highness by the time I was seriously writing. And by that time I had a gang of young people—including brilliant young men like Wynton Marsalis and Stanley Crouch—and I was the old man for them. At this time I was visualizing myself as Royal Highness looking back, thinking, in other words, what would I have told them at sixty-five?

JS: Well, timing is important for a writer—

AM: You know, you can project forward as well as back. And I look at those old people in Thomas Mann's *Buddenbrooks,* which he wrote at 25, and those old people come off just as well.

JS: Sure. And with feeling—
AM: That's right.

JS: Well, I think that the time in which we now see Scooter in *The Spyglass Tree* is not simply his involvement at the college level. There are flashbacks that take him home. *The Spyglass Tree,* we should tell our viewers, is based on the chinaberry tree that was out in the front yard of this little three-room shotgun house where Scooter lived. But the scenes there and the life experiences there come across with vivid reality for me. I think politics in the barbershop is politics the world over.

AM: Um hmm.

JS: I think two young roommates—male—talking about sex or experimenting with sex or Scooter talking with Little Buddy Marshall about Creola—I think that's a universal conversation.

AM: Right.

JS: And in a real sense those scenes in which Scooter reminisces about Miss Tee and about Mama, those are universal experiences, at least I think for southerners who look back.

AM: Right. I aspire to make it work on those levels so we get the romance of the south, and how can you have romance without dragons? Just because they're Grand Dragons doesn't mean that they're not dragons—

JS: [Laughs.] We've got a little of that in there too, you know—
AM: But what is a medieval romance except a guy going out to slay

dragons? So if you lose sight of the heroic dimension that you should aspire to—now what I've done is bootleg in there by way of sheer Albert Murray effort—is that the blues idiom is a philosophical context within which you define this action and also where you define your aspiration and your quest for adventure. While complaining that there are difficulties out there, you forge your sword and you go get it. That's what the blues are: You've got negative lyrics that tell a tale of woe, which tell you about failure and disappointment and being double-crossed, but you affirm life by stomping the blues away. In the face of spelling out a tale of woe, you move from a purification ritual into a celebration of life. Nothing is more aphrodisiastic than the blues. You don't play the blues in a church or at a prayer meeting. You play it when you're going to get down and have barbecue, and have your best clothes on and your best girl—

JS: And a little booze and a little dance, that's right—

AM: And you look at that and you have to improvise in the face of it. So a disjuncture in this mythology is not trauma-producing, it's a break. And on the break you do your thing. So at the center of that is heroic action at all times. And Scooter is geared to all of that. And he runs it through all of these various levels, academic levels of heroism and stories and so forth, but he comes back home, back downhome, to this idiomatic frame, and he tries to enrich that by his awareness. And I think it's legitimate because he's a college student; students can be very artificial about this if they want to, and it would be perfectly natural that they would deal with essays literally in that way.

JS: It's very difficult I think to have a hero in the classic sense without danger.

AM: That's right.

JS: You introduce Scooter to that physical world of jeopardy through three people, Will Spradley, Dudley Philpot, and Giles Cunningham. Spradley takes a terrible beating from Philpot. Philpot threatens Giles Cunningham, a stolid, forceful, dynamic figure with a great sense of security.

AM: So he projects other vibes altogether—

JS: Absolutely.

AM: And Scooter is in touch with more quality than this guy Philpot.

JS: That's exactly right. And Dudley Philpot in the final analysis makes the threat but doesn't have the guts to follow through on the threat. But in the process of that Scooter learns that he has the stuff and joins with Giles Cunningham to protect him against whatever.

AM: The whole thing could have been wiped out. All that "early bird," "talented tenth," and so forth could have been wiped out. But he had to face the fact that that is the jeopardy. It's like being prepared for a hurricane, or a volcano, or whatever—because that's a part of life.

In literature you have two types of statements that Kenneth Burke likes to talk about—they're terribly important to me—and I used to teach them to my students: You can set up a frame of acceptance or a frame of rejection. Now what you accept is the necessity of struggle. And it's out of that literary strategy that you get the epic. The frame of rejection is a lamentation, the elegy—you bemoan the sorry fate of man. People mistake the blues in that sense. The blues are a frame of acceptance. The sociologists will make you think it's a frame of rejection—moaning and commiserating. But really they're stomping the blues away and they're going to get it on.

JS: Would the spiritual connote lamentation?

AM: The spiritual is another thing. That's a sacred mode so genuflection is the thing with the spiritual.

Honor for a Writer Who Puts Blues in His Words

Stephan Salisbury / 1992

From *The Philadelphia Inquirer,* February 14, 1992, p. D1. Reprinted with permission from The Philadelphia Inquirer.

Albert Murray is a little slow afoot these days, hobbled by bum circulation in his right leg. But sit him down in a decent chair and lob a question, and Murray scoots and riffs, races and roams from Thomas Mann to Duke Ellington to fairy tales to *Finnegans Wake* and back again.

No boundaries in Murray's world; nothing is off-limits to his inquiry.

"What I'm concerned with," he said, "is what are the sources or the achievements of man's effort to understand his sojourn on the earth? What has the human mind produced anywhere in the world that contributes to this?"

Murray has been called "one of the best-kept secrets in American literature."

The secret seems to be getting out.

Now 75, and the author of a sheaf of novels and essays that have, among other things, helped transform jazz criticism and reordered the musical cosmology, Murray is at last being recognized as one of this country's preeminent writers.

At a 6 p.m. reception tomorrow at the Free Library, 19th and Vine Streets, Murray will be honored for a lifetime of literary achievement. He'll also moderate a panel on the state of black writing at 2 p.m. at the Community College of Philadelphia, 17th and Spring Garden Streets.

The ceremony and panel are part of the eighth annual Celebration of Black Writing, a two-day series of panel discussions, readings and informal book talk sponsored by Moonstone Inc., a nonprofit educational organization.

Gimpy leg or no, Murray will be down for the action, taking time from a slew of projects, including a video documentary on Count Basie, a Smithsonian Institution project on Duke Ellington, a Lincoln Center Jazz series, another novel.

Although his work has been widely praised in music circles, broader recognition has been slow in coming. At least in part, Murray believes this is due to the uncompromising intellectual core of his work. Everything he writes—whether memoir, novel or critical essay—is of a piece, stitched together with the same tough ideas. His work is endlessly inventive and vivid.

"I'm trying to solve a damn problem that doesn't appeal to people unless they're really serious or really disturbed," said Murray. "That's the way I feel. But it's the only thing worth doing."

Most of that effort relates in some fashion to jazz, Murray's touchstone, his inspiration and alembic, what he has called "the great American achievement." With jazz and the blues, "you're talking about relative ways of getting at the truth," he said, discussing his attraction to music.

"That's the art form that has given the most comprehensive and sophisticated representation of black experience in America. I couldn't find that in the literature, in the books, because they were mainly concerned with justice and injustice. . . .

"What I wanted to do was to find a literary equivalent of the blues. You spell that out, and you've got a whole frame of reference—intellectual frame of reference—which allows you to write an American literature, not just black literature."

In his first book, *The Omni-Americans* (1970), a collection of closely argued essays, Murray explores ideas of American identity, presenting black American culture as endlessly inventive, catholic and open to possibility. In the autobiographical *South to a Very Old Place* (1972), he elaborates on the idea of culture-as-jam-session, culture as a continuously evolving blend of high and low, learned and vernacular.

His books on jazz and the blues—*The Hero and the Blues* (1973) and *Stomping the Blues* (1976)—present an extended metaphor of music as an emblem of heroic creation. Blues music is not a respite from suffering but is a transcendence.

"The blues as such are synonymous with low spirits," he writes in *Stomping the Blues*. "Blues music is not. With all of its so-called blue notes and overtones of sadness, blues music of its very nature and function is nothing if not a form of diversion. . . . Not only is its express purpose to make people feel good, which is to say in high spirits, but in the process of doing so it is actually expected to generate a disposition that is both elegantly playful and heroic in its nonchalance."

"My whole thing is to deal with jazz as fine art," said Murray. "You're not going to show me anybody who was a greater 20th-century American

composer than Duke Ellington. You sure ain't goin' to bring me a George
Gershwin or Aaron Copland or (Charles) Ives. None of these guys have the
appeal."

This feisty man with the neat mustache and graying hair chatted for several
hours the other day, forgetting all about his lame leg. During the conversation, he sat at his desk, which looks south over Harlem rooftops, and repeatedly bobbed up to pluck a pertinent book from the shelves lining the living
room.

At one point, he pulled down three volumes of Frederick Douglass' work;
at another, he pulled out Alec Wilder's *Popular American Song*; at another,
a scholarly journal with a Murray essay; at another, he opened a box and
unveiled a vast compendium of clippings compiled for *Good Morning Blues*
(1985), Count Basie's autobiography, which Murray wrote.

Not only does Murray's sense of form and culture derive from his close
study of music, but his prose style, supple and rich, full of cross-rhythms,
calls Duke Ellington and Sidney Bechet and Louis Armstrong vividly to
mind. This is especially true of his two novels, *Train Whistle Guitar* (1974)
and *The Spyglass Tree* (1991), about growing up in the Deep South in the
'20s and '30s.

And sometimes Murray's conversation just falls into syncopation—a beating of rhythms, a scatting, a humming echo of Duke or Count.

"It turned out that when I moved closer in [to study jazz] that the content
of it had implications that were terrific," he said. "When I looked at the
[musical] break, I realized, since I'm interested in fairy tales and myth, where
that fits into heroic action. I understood 'moment of truth'—all these literary
conceptions."

He stopped, mid-idea, and began to thump out a rhythm on his desk and
the cover of an old Smith-Corona.

Dom-ticky-dom-ticky-dom-ticky-dom-ticky-DOMP!

"Is that supposed to be trauma-producing?" Murray said, chuckling. "Or
is that the time when you write your signature on the epidermis of actuality?
You see? It's called a break. That's your break. Isn't that interesting? It has
both meanings. It's a break that can produce a trauma, a fish out of water,
because, see, the cadence is interrupted."

He thumps again, rattling the Smith-Corona, scatting.

"Dom-ticky-dom-ticky-dom-ticky-dom-ticky-DOMP!"

"This music was my music," he said. "The music from the idiom in which

I grew up, that I knew about; the music that impinged most intimately on my everyday experience," he said. "I had to deal with all the dimension ad-dressed in the music. To do that, I had to come to terms with all of American society."

The Unsquarest Person Duke Ellington Ever Met

Mark Feeney / 1993

From *The Boston Globe Magazine,* August 1, 1993, pp. 15, 28–33.
Reprinted courtesy of The Boston Globe.

It's a Saturday afternoon, and sunlight fills Albert Murray's study. He refers to his vantage high above Harlem as "my spyglass tree," a phrase he savors— *The Spyglass Tree* being the title of his most recent book—and the window by his desk affords a panoramic view of the midtown skyline, four miles to the south. Yet the items Murray has brought out to show a visitor— scrapbooks, photo albums, folders of correspondence—are as spectacular in their way as the Manhattan skyscrapers. They are two-dimensional products of a vigorously three-dimensional life led at the intersection of literature and music, intellect and culture, race and consciousness in 20th-century America.

Ralph Ellison looks dreamy in a snapshot Murray took at a picnic in the '30s. In another picture, Murray confers with James Baldwin in Paris in 1950. Other photos show Murray backstage with Duke Ellington, between sets with Count Basie, greeting Wynton Marsalis. There are letters from Ellison, Robert Penn Warren, Langston Hughes, Joseph Campbell—and one from a former White House aide, recounting how he overheard an appreciative Lyndon Johnson read aloud the appraisal of LBJ in Murray's book *South to a Very Old Place.*

Around the corner, a large lithograph by another friend of Murray's, Romare Bearden, faces floor-to-ceiling shelves filled with first editions of Hemingway and Faulkner, Thomas Mann and T. S. Eliot, André Malraux and W. H. Auden. Auden is a particular favorite, and over the course of an afternoon Murray will emphasize points by quoting from memory snatches of his poetry, as well as passages from Edna St. Vincent Millay, e. e. cummings, and Marianne Moore. The words tumble out as if part of an endless tutorial. One of the planet's champion talkers, Murray is a born teacher. As another longtime friend, Charlie Davidson, owner of The Andover Shop, in Harvard Square, approvingly notes, "He'd like to educate the whole human race." And Murray is happy to use any means available: one minute reciting Mod-

70

ernist verse, the next singing a chorus of "Going to Chicago"—and delivering it with an insouciance someone a third his age (Murray turned 77 this spring) would be hard pressed to match.

Albert Murray is "what a man of letters should and could be," says the novelist John Edgar Wideman. "He represents the best in thought and writing." Walker Percy speculated that Murray's essay collection, *The Omni-Americans,* published in 1970, "well may be the most important book on black-white relations in the United States, indeed on American culture, published in this generation." Or there is what Ellington wrote about his friend 20 years ago, when Murray's first novel, *Train Whistle Guitar,* was published: "He doesn't have to look it up. . . . If you want to know, look him up. He is the unsquarest person I know." Short of having the pope call you the holiest person *he* knows, it's hard to imagine a more authoritative order of praise.

Indeed, those who know Murray tend to be passionate in their admiration. Yet the size of his reputation is incommensurate with its quality. It's unlikely you have heard of Albert Murray, or, if you have, that you know his work in all its aspects. A reader who prizes Murray's two novels may never have heard of his *Stomping the Blues,* which the critic Stanley Crouch has called "the most eloquent book ever written about African-American music." Those who esteem him as the *eminence grise* of the well-known music series Jazz at Lincoln Center or know him as Count Basie's collaborator might not be acquainted with *The Omni-Americans.* Laments Rob Gibson, director of Jazz at Lincoln Center, "It's amazing to me how unrecognized Al Murray is in terms of the grand scheme of things."

That lack of recognition has various roots: a fondness for controversy, a delight in idiosyncratic views, an unwillingness to settle for any one literary niche, and a career path so roundabout that, well, as the saying goes, "only in America." Murray is as close to a classic 19th-century man of letters as one might find in this country today—except that few men of letters wait until age 54 to publish their first book; spend 15 years in the military; and, not to put too fine a point on it, are black. Murray has suffered for his singularity.

When white intellectuals "see a dark-skinned person," Murray explains, "they want you to be belly-aching. They don't want you to be explaining things as if you're smarter than they are. You're going to explain Malraux, you're going to explain Hemingway . . . the guy wants to know, 'How did you happen to read that?' Now, that's an insulting question. I went to school!"

The last thing to expect from Murray is belly-aching. Among his central tenets are a belief in the advantage of adversity—"That's what the blues are trying to say: Look at adversity as opportunity. . . . I'm trying to find the literary equivalent for all that"—and honoring what he calls the "ancestral imperative." That means living up to the standards set for us by previous generations, and in such a context belly-aching is a form of betrayal. "There's nobody in the United States that's had the heroic requirements of black people," Murray points out, and aspiration is the only response worthy of their heroism.

"Here they are, a whole generation that looks upon themselves as victims. Nobody's caring about the ancestral imperatives of Frederick Douglass, Harriet Tubman. Don't tell me about no goddamn role model. Who was Frederick Douglass' role model? See, that's social-science cliche. Who was George Washington's role model? Who was Abraham Lincoln's role model? That's a cliche from a course somewhere that somebody got tenure on. If you have a role model, you got one—but who was his? So if you don't have one, you make one."

Murray bridles when asked if such talk might be labeled conservative. "You can't solve problems with epithets," he replies. Murray belongs to no political camp. In *The Omni-Americans,* he made plain his distaste for what he calls the "politics of unexamined slogans," and that remains true today. Back in the late '60s, when received opinion held that blacks were simply whites with darker skins ("Why can't they be more like us?" was the cocktail-party complaint), Murray was arguing for the vitality of differences between blacks and whites and how those differences make an essential contribution to a common American culture. Twenty-five years later, when received opinion holds that blacks are oppressed by the concept of a single American culture ("Why *shouldn't* they be less like us?" activists ask), Murray emphasizes an American commonality.

Having once reproached whites with the rejoinder "We're all in this together," he does not shy away from addressing it to blacks. "You hear a lot of this bullshit about people backing off of being Eurocentric: That's the only thing we *can* be! You have Greenwich mean time, and everybody goes to it, so might as well not argue with it. I mean, this is 1993, right? I don't care if you're in Latin America or New Zealand, we're all in 1993. The whole earth is Eurocentric. And it's not a good thing or a bad thing—it's *the* thing. . . . The Japanese don't feel they have to be Nippocentric. They can be more

Eurocentric than the Europeans; trying to make better automobiles than the Europeans, better sound equipment. . . ."

"Diversity" is an essential concept to Murray, but his interpretation differs from the one most common today. In that view, diversity is inelastic and compartmentalized (blacks are here, whites there, Latinos somewhere else, and so on, with space demarcated for each). Dismissing that as "neo-segrega-tionism," Murray sees a diversity predicated on fluidity, and he celebrates American society as a whole rather than any of its constitutive parts. He made this argument most memorably in *The Omni-Americans: "American culture, even in its most rigidly segregated precincts, is patently and irrevo-cably composite. It is, regardless of all the hysterical protestations of those who would have it otherwise, incontestably mulatto* [Murray's italics]. In-deed, for all their traditional antagonisms and obvious differences, the so-called black and so-called white people in the United States resemble nobody else in the world so much as they resemble each other. And what is more, even their most extreme and violent polarities represent nothing so much as the natural history of pluralism in an open society."

There's something in that paragraph to offend everyone: black and white, liberal and conservative, multi-culturalist and majoritarian. Far more impor-tant, it offers a profound and thrilling vision—of America as improvisational stew, as an ecstasy of admixture—that is worthy of Lincoln at his noblest, Whitman at his grandest, Louis Armstrong at his most spectacular.

Indeed, each American is, almost by definition, an individuated coalition in his or her daily actions: speaking the queen's English, eating a smorgas-bord of ethnic cuisines, listening to African-derived music on the latest Asian technology. The question of what it means to be *American*—a condition that subsumes everything from William Faulkner's sentence structure to Duke Ellington's chord progressions to, not least of all, the matter of how a "Remus-derived, book-oriented downhome boy" got from a neighborhood in Alabama called Magazine Point to membership in New York's prestigious Century Association—informs almost everything Murray has written.

Growing up on the outskirts of Mobile, Albert Murray knew a world that was at once intensely parochial—marked by such colorful names as Gin's Alley, Chickasabogue Creek, No Man's Land—and surprisingly cosmopolitan. From Pullman porters and black World War I veterans, there were tales of cities far away. Murray and his friends took pride in such heroes as the young

Satchel Paige (who often pitched in Mobile) and the blues singers who would appear at local juke joints. From early on, a sense of style was imbued.

Something far more important than style, the ancestral imperative, was imbued at Mobile County Training School. Under its principal, Benjamin Francis Baker, MCTS taught its students to excel. "Be the answer to the old folks' prayer," Murray and his schoolmates were urged, and 60 years later the respect in his voice is audible when he speaks of "the ingenuity and the assiduity that Mr. Baker put into the mission of making the school second to none."

A top student, Murray was quarterback on the football team and captained the basketball squad (though "that was another era of basketball," he admits). It was never in doubt that he'd go on to college; MCTS "had that 'talented tenth' orientation," Murray recalls, using W. E. B. Du Bois' term for black America's best and brightest and the need for them to strive and achieve. "The smartest students were earmarked for the best schools. . . . But it was hard to get me to Brown or to Harvard or to some place like that, because we just didn't have the money." So instead, with a "scholarship voucher and no return ticket," Murray went off to Tuskegee Institute, in Alabama.

Tuskegee was the most famous of the historically black colleges and the richest. It exemplified the lessons Murray had learned at MCTS about pride and achievement. At Tuskegee, he met an upperclassman named Ralph Ellison; a shared interest in literature and music led to a friendship that continues today. Indeed, that interest made them allies as well as friends. "You couldn't be pretentious," Murray says, "because that wouldn't impress anybody! At Howard or Fisk, taking humanities, you could put on airs. But when you opened your mouth around those guys [at Tuskegee], you had to make sense. Ralph and I laugh about that all the time."

Graduating in 1939, Murray returned to Tuskegee a year later to teach composition and literature. A photograph from that time would seem to suggest that the young instructor, who in his 70s remains a notably handsome man, must have cut a considerable figure with the coeds. "Uh-huh," he laughs, "and I got me the prettiest." Her name was Mozelle Menefee. Two years ago she and Murray celebrated their 50th wedding anniversary. Their only child, Michele, is a former Alvin Ailey dancer.

During World War II, Murray's service in the Army Air Force gave new meaning to the term "military academy." "We used to take the AT6, the advanced trainer that was available for weekend cross-country flights, and I would get guys to go to New York, you see? I'd come back with a musette bag full of books from the Gotham Book Mart."

That education resumed when the Korean War saw him called back to active duty in 1951, after he'd already earned a master's degree from New York University. Murray spent four years supervising the ROTC program at Tuskegee, then was transferred to Morocco. "It wasn't an interruption from my writing career," he notes of the Air Force. "I had more time to read. Tolstoy pointed out that literary people flourish in the military. You have a lot of free time. You get to travel. You can practice foreign languages. When I was shipped to Morocco, I bought my Leica and wanted to check it out, so I got a space-available flight and went to Athens and shot the Parthenon. I could go to Rome. I went to Istanbul. How? Because I was in the Air Force."

After Morocco, Murray served at Long Beach, California, and then Hans-com Field, in Bedford. Every Saturday he'd go into Harvard Square to check out the bookstores and drop in at The Andover Shop, where he and Charlie Davidson formed a circle that included newspaper columnist George Frazier, jazz impresario George Wein, and, whenever they were in town, cabaret singer Bobby Short and composer Alec Wilder, who would later recommend Murray as co-author for Count Basie's memoirs.

Murray retired in 1962 with the rank of major and moved to New York. With time out for an occasional visiting professorship (he has taught at Co-lumbia, Colgate, Emory, and the University of Massachusetts at Boston), he has concentrated on his writing ever since. Being in New York also deepened his friendship with Ellington, whom Murray had first met backstage at Carne-gie Hall in 1946. "We got very close. I went to all his recording sessions. He'd say, 'You're going to be free Thursday, right? Well, we can set up a flight for you to come out to LA Thursday night, and you really don't have to get back until Tuesday.' So he'd set it up, have everything ready, pick up the expenses. Those were the kind of terms we were on."

It was as "an older man and better writer" that Murray started to publish. As if to make up for lost time, his first four books appeared in rapid succes-sion. Two years after *The Omni-Americans* came out, *South to a Very Old Place* (1972) was nominated for a National Book Award in nonfiction. The next year saw publication of *The Hero and the Blues,* then *Train Whistle Guitar* (1974), which won the Lillian Smith Award for Southern Fiction, and *Stomping the Blues* (1976).

If anything, Murray has gotten younger in his prose as he has gotten older in his years, and his most recent book, *The Spyglass Tree* (1991), is the most vigorously written. Continuing the tale of Scooter, the autobiographical hero of *Train Whistle Guitar,* it is full of loose talk and tall tales (the titular tree doubles as beanstalk) that take the reader South to a very vivid place.

The musicality of his writing is such that, in some ways, Murray's style is best seen (or, rather, heard) alongside not another writer's but that of the great Ellington trumpeter Cootie Williams or Basie trombonist Al Grey: players with a highly vocal approach to their horns, full of smears and slurs and growls. Murray's writing is replete with shouts and squalls and snickers, a voice equally given to Joycean word play and gutbucket formulations. It's a gorgeous, flaunting, rumbustious, rhythm-a-ning prose that curls and sprawls and edges sideways—like everyday human speech, only calmer, livelier, lighter on its feet.

After *Stomping the Blues,* it took Murray 10 years to publish his next book, and, technically, it wasn't even his. Count Basie's autobiography, *Good Morning Blues* (1986), turned into a highly labor-intensive labor of love, one that required countless hours of interviewing and research as well as writing. Still, it was an ideal match of authors. As Basie told his manager after a get-acquainted lunch with Murray, "I hope you can get him, because that's the way I would talk if I could talk."

Murray has always been able to talk the language of jazz musicians, and today he's talking with a new generation of them through his membership on the committee for the Jazz at Lincoln Center program, in New York City. "He's the overriding, grandfather figure for the program—an aesthetic presence," notes its director, Rob Gibson. The mission of Jazz at Lincoln Center is to encourage an appreciation for the music's past and, in doing so, enhance and expand the music's present and future. An aesthetic variation on the ancestral imperative, it's something close to Murray's heart.

"See," he says, "what the Lincoln Center thing tries to do is establish the responsibility to the canon. If you say you got an art form, then what makes up the art form? What should you be able to do? You know what to do if you're talking about European concert-hall music. If you're a piano player, there's a literature of the piano you should know about. It doesn't stop you from becoming Stravinsky or Hindemith or Satie or Debussy. But they know that other stuff. Jazz should have its canon; they should know that. Whereas these people have been rolling up the carpet. The journalists who, to promote bop, put down New Orleans music as 'Dixieland,' 'moldy fig,' stuff like that. So those people cut themselves off from all that. They put you into this category, into that category, as if it all weren't yours.

"It's the old thing of T. S. Eliot's 'Tradition and the Individual Talent.' You stand up there, you got four bars, but everything should be in there. Everything. Your knowledge of that is still there, even when you're leaving it out, as Hemingway would say. It's that type of responsibility."

Lincoln Center is only one of many tasks currently keeping Murray busy. He was a judge for this year's Robert F. Kennedy Book Award and in the fall will be DuPont Visiting Professor at Washington and Lee University, in Virginia. Two books await publication—an essay collection and a study of Hemingway—and he's 400 pages into his third novel.

Asked if there'll be a fourth book about Scooter, Murray has a ready reply: "Depends on my condition!" For all his young-kid energy, he owns up to having slowed down some. Murray is a bit hard of hearing and walks with a cane, the result of an arthritic knee and two operations last year. "They went in and had to remove a vertebra here"—he points to his neck. "Every now and then there's a little clonking. But I have some young friends who clonk, too, when you normally clank, so I guess I'm all right." His knowing eyes will get a faraway look sometimes, but a splendid, complicit grin rapidly dispels the distance. The "very nice boy full of mischievousness," as Murray describes his alter ego, Scooter, remains easy enough to discern in the 77-year-old man.

Some discern other possibilities there, too. Charlie Davidson, for one, sees a presidential adviser. "I used to fantasize that one of the presidents would be told about Al," he says, "and no matter what the problem is . . . he'd turn to him and say, 'Al, what do *you* think?' I mean, really, imagine some square like George Bush saying, 'Al, what's this thing here?' . . . He'd be so good with someone like Bush! He'd say, 'George, that's the way it *is!*' "

Laying down the law in the Oval Office? It doesn't seem likely (even today, with a president who grew up fantasizing about playing tenor with Thelonious Monk). But few things in Murray's life have seemed likely, and that hasn't kept him from accomplishing them. "The most radical thing that you can do," he says, "is to be a nice-looking, brown-skinned American guy, well dressed, well educated; that's the most dangerous sonofabitch in the country!" Saying those words, this nice-looking, brown-skinned American guy, well dressed and well educated, doesn't appear very dangerous (for starters, he's got a smile on his face), but you can see what he means.

Albert Murray on Stage:
An Interview
Louis Edwards / 1994

Originally published in *((speak my name)): Black Men on Masculinity and the American Dream* (New York: Beacon Press, 1995), pp. 42–58. Reprinted with the permission of Louis Edwards. Copyright by Louis Edwards.

Albert Murray, born in 1916, is a grand surviving griot from a prodigious generation that includes writers Ralph Ellison, John A. Williams, and Ernest Gaines. He is a cultural critic (*The Omni-Americans* [1970], *The Hero and the Blues* [1973], *Stomping the Blues* [1976]) and a fiction writer (*Train Whistle Guitar* [1974], *The Spyglass Tree* [1990]). Louis Edwards is as gifted a young writer as can be drawn from a new generation of writers re-creating the story of black male witness in America. His first novel, *Ten Seconds* (1991), was hailed by critics and fellow writers alike. Edwards, born in 1962, has already won the prestigious Whiting Writer's Award and is completing a new novel. The following conversation, in part inscribing the living ritual of black, male mentorship, took place on July 13, 1994, in Murray's Harlem apartment, where he lives with his wife and daughter.

Edwards: I'd like to begin with a discussion of *The Omni-Americans,* not just because it's the beginning of your publishing history, but because it's *such* a beginning and such a way to hear your voice for the first time. So how did that book come about? Talk about the political and literary climates at the time—late sixties, early seventies—and about how the book was received.

Murray: Well, it was obviously a book that was stimulated by the civil rights movement. And it had to do with what I thought was basic—that is, the question of identity and who these people were and how they saw themselves in the actions that they were participating in. To me it's always a matter of context and a matter of the broadest possible human context. So I wanted to define what it meant to be an American, and how we fit into it, and I came up with the idea that we're *fundamental* to it—that you can't be an American unless you're part *us,* just as you can't be an American unless you're part *them.* I came up with the concept of a culture that as a context makes for, literally and figuratively speaking, a mulatto culture. I was thinking the whole time I was writing *The Omni-Americans* about "all-American," but I couldn't use that term because I didn't want to get confused with that term as it's used in athletics. But it means "all-American." "Omni-Americans" means "all-Americans." America is interwoven with all these different strains. The subtitle of that section of the book is "E Pluribus Unum"—one out of many. Whether you want to get all tangled up in "melting pot" or "glorious mosaic" or any of those phrases is another thing. It just means that people are interwoven, and they represent what Constance Rourke calls a composite. Then you can start defining individuals in their variations, but they're in that context and they can only define themselves in that context. They're in a position where they're the heirs of all the culture of all the ages. Because of innovations in communication and transportation, the ideas of people all over the world and people of different epochs impinge upon us, on part of our consciousness.

Edwards: Then the term "omni-Americans" applies not just to African-Americans, but to all Americans, and to—well, maybe not to all people, but perhaps we're discussing "omni-humanity."

Murray: Yes. Absolutely. We're looking for universality. We're looking for the common ground of man. And what you're doing when you separate the American from all of that, is you're talking about *idiomatic* identity. You see? And if you go from culture, instead of the impossibility of race . . . because you can't *define* race. It doesn't meet our intellectual standard with a scientific observation and definition and whatever. It won't meet it! You see, race is an ideological concept. It has to do with manipulating people, and with power, and with controlling people in a certain way. It has no reality, no basis in reality. Because, see, if you try to make a genetic definition—"has this gene, has that gene"—how many of this gene or these genes or those genes would it take to make you white or black or yellow or brown or red, if you use this crude ratio? Now how do you determine who has that many, and where's the line of demarcation? It's an *impossible* situation. So what you enter into to make sense of things are patterns and variations in culture. What you find are variations we can call idiomatic—idiomatic variations. People do the same things, have the same basic human impulses, but they come out differently. The language changes because of the environment and so forth. Now, you can get the environment, you can get the cultural elements, and from those things you can predict the behavior of people fairly well. But if you look at such racial characteristics as may be used—whether it's the shape of certain body parts, the texture of the hair, the lips, and all—you cannot get a scientific correlation between how the guy looks and how he behaves. If you find a large number of people who look like each other and behave like each other, it's because of the culture. Because there are too many other variations. If you've got guys from stovepipe black to snow blond, you're going to find all the variations in mankind, even though idiomatically they might speak the same, they might *sound* the same.

Edwards: The ideas that you espoused in *The Omni-Americans,* were they considered radical? I mean, there are those who would say this is wrong even today. The social scientists would still argue with you.

Murray: But they're segregationists. I make the point in *The Omni-Americans* that nobody is more dependent upon segregation than the social scientist.

Edwards: It's his work.

Murray: That's why I call social science as used in America a folklore of white supremacy and a *fake*lore of black pathology. Anything that black people do is abnormal. If it's good, it's still abnormal. So if you're well conditioned, like superstar basketball players, it's because there's something wrong with you. Any other time when you're discussing such matters, if you've got these things together, if you're discharging the emotional thing that your system is healthier, if you're laughing and you're making jokes and you're playing around, then you're automatically, by any other definition of psychiatry and so forth, you're happier and you're on better terms with life. But then somebody will say something is wrong with you if you're not angry enough—which is a pathological condition. Even if you're in the face of danger, you're still in an abnormal functioning of the body because you're confronted with danger, but it's not the most desired state of human existence. You've got that balance between a perception of jeopardy and a technology for coping with it *and* a sense of the ridiculousness and a sense of the futility or the emptiness, after all, of it. Because once you get to be good enough at science, you're linked up with particles and waves! [Laughter.]

So then all you've got left are metaphors, and those metaphors had better be adequate. And they're adequate if they add up to the possibility of dynamic equilibrium which brings a sense of fulfillment and therefore happiness.

Edwards: Well, many of your metaphors have, I think, serious political implications and resonance, but they do not read that way. They don't read as politics. They read more as philosophy.

Murray: Well, it's a human thing.

Edwards: Back to the search for universal humanity.

Murray: Let me give you an analogy, a rough Murray analogy. If you went to the athletic department of a college . . . you have one guy who is a coach of the basketball team, the track team, and another guy who is a physical director. He teaches physical education, he conditions the body for all those other things. If you do well enough, if you can pass all of that, then you might be a basketball player, you might be a track guy—the application of the conditioning. In other words, if our humanities, if our metaphors, if our arts are adequate, then our ideals and aspirations will be adequate. It wouldn't be just a matter of food, clothing, and shelter. It would be a human transcendence that goes beyond that, that takes you beyond our conception of what animal or plant life is. It's those ideas or those images of human possibility that make for aspiration, that make for a sense of achievement— and a sense of failure. So you've got literature right there. If you get a wrong definition of what the objectives are, if you go for material things—just go for money, or just for power—you will then cause a lot of confusion and it won't be adding toward the thing that you really want, which is that dynamic equilibrium, which is always precarious, but which makes for what we call happiness, which is very, very delicate at all times. It has to be watched at all times because it changes. But it's what we want. We know it when we get it.

Edwards: The requirements to bring about happiness change.

Murray: You've got to have a sense of actual achievement. One of the things about my writing that I want to make people conscious of is the underlying ritual that's there. That's what keeps them informed that I'm going to be applying this to politics, I'm going to be applying this to this type of administration. But you've got a vision of life which is adequate, so that it enriches your political program, your political position, or what you *want*.

Count Basie and I were working on his book, and when we got near the end we started looking through collections of pictures. At one point there—I guess just before he was leaving Kansas City to come to New York—there's a picture of him and he has a gold tooth in the front of his mouth. And when I saw this picture I said, "Hey, Count. What happened to that gold tooth?" He looked at the picture and he said, "I didn't know what to want." Isn't that terrific? "I didn't know what to want." When he got more hip, he took that thing out; he had beautiful teeth that went so well with his complexion and all.

Edwards: That's a great story.

Murray: We're talking about the political implications of what I was doing. . . . It was a matter of laying an adequate foundation, so that whatever you do on top of it would be adequate.

Edwards: Now, one of the most complex works that you've written would be *South to a Very Old Place*—in my opinion—which, I'll admit, I had a hard time fully comprehending. I realize that there is a very intricate pattern that is at work there. Could you discuss what you were up to? I think it might help people approach that work.

Murray: *The Omni-Americans* would be a discussion where I'm wearing the hat of the intellectual, where I'm trying to set up the issues and address basic questions. *South to a Very Old Place* tries to be a work of art, where the actions and the pictures have their own application. If you give people a legend, they want a picture. If you give them a picture, they want a legend. If you wear two hats, as a novelist and an intellectual, you do them both. As a college teacher, I could do them both. I wanted to be an artist. I tried my best to make *South to a Very Old Place* a work of art.

Edwards: It's clearly that.

Murray: I wanted it to be read for the pleasure of how it is written, and then all of that stuff is all loaded. You can say all kinds of things that mean all kinds of things, and it's all in focus if you get the art working for you. With the hocus-pocus you make it swing, and then you get all the other stuff. You want to make the ineffable articulate. So you're in an interesting area there, and when you get to *Train Whistle,* there's an attempt to give you the clue . . . "the also and the also" of this or that; you should get the whole. "Also and also" is the ultimate implication, the personal, the local, the world-wide implications. The also and the also: *etcetera.* It's endless.

That's like music again. I start with real fundamentals. Entropy. So when I'm writing about the blues, it's the whole philosophical system right there. What's the blues? Entropy. The tendency of all phenomena to become random, to fall apart. It's chaos. That's what's so devastating about the blues. So what you've got to do is superimpose a form on that. That's why I can make jazz and the jazz musician central to my whole literary, philosophical system of American identity, because we simply are the stars of [that system], the touchstone of it. I can do a Lester Young take-off on Jefferson. I can do a Cootie Williams or Louis Armstrong thing on Lincoln. I can do all this. You can play with all that stuff and make it feel right even if you can't articulate it yet. It's that type of thing. And nobody's come up with an image of the American that I think is richer in possibility and more consistent with the assumptions underlying the social contract that we live in terms of.

Edwards: Are you saying or implying that the order in which you've published your work is part of an overall plan or scheme? Because from *The Omni-Americans* to *South to a Very Old Place* to *Train Whistle Guitar*—I think *The Hero and the Blues* may be in between the two latter works—the works all flow into one another. Or is that serendipity?

Murray: Well, in a sense. . . . When I got into the pieces that add up to *The Omni-Americans,* I realized I was writing on a theme, the theme of identity. The title of the book has to do with identity. We're the all-Americans. We symbolize that more than anything else. It's a mulatto culture. Boom! You can just play all kinds of changes. You can write fifteen-hundred-page books on that stuff. But what I'd been doing was thinking though the whole thing and I had really written *The Hero and the Blues* first. That's what I was working on when the assignments that would become *The Omni-Americans* started coming in, so I had the context. I had the intellectual frame of reference. I was working it out, working on an aesthetic. So when I started writing these pieces, I knew I was writing a book, because it was inside a context. I wanted to deal with the richest possible context, and what came out was all I knew about literature, all this stuff on my shelves. When I was ready to open up, there I was writing a book! You know, "Thomas Mann, who said this and this . . ." I was gone! I knew where I was going on that. Then I get that *e pluribus unum,* how far back you go. . . .

If I were not so realistic and didn't have to face the tragic dimension of life—as well as life's farcical dimension—I would be very much depressed. Too many of the black intellectuals have been unable to address the first fifteen pages of *The Omni-Americans.* I enter history at the middle point in the Middle Passage. My work sets up a cultural and intellectual context in which we can define ourselves as Americans—second to none. Any African who jumped overboard en route to the New World is not my ancestor, because what we do has to do with survival in this state. You don't have a better prototype for the self-created American than Harriet Tubman, Frederick Douglass, or Louis Armstrong picking up that horn. My work establishes the basis of our American identity. . . . And that's where the necessity of swing begins. Eternal resilience. Perpetual creativity. . . . So by the time I got into *The Omni-Americans,* I was going. It *had* to be a book. Then you feed in these other things which I was dealing with at the time—jazz, literature, style. I would just bounce them against a frame of reference. That's how *The Omni-Americans* came to be.

But when you get to *South to a Very Old Place,* that started out as an assignment for a series that Willie Morris was running at *Harper's* magazine, called "Going Home in America." Some people would go to the midwest; some people would go to this place, that place. He asked me to do one and I decided to go south. Then I started playing with irony immediately. Go north. Go north this way, go north that way. Go north and south. Then to be sure you get it, you've got Joyce, you've got Mann, you've got all these people to help you. So you put Christopher Columbus there and say, "He went east by going west; I'm going south by going north." You're playing with all these things if you're a contemporary writer. You've got to write as if all these people exist.

Edwards [laughing]: That leads to another question I have. I want you to talk about some of the very significant relationships you've had with some of the great black male artists of this century.

Murray: What do all these guys have in common? What do Ellison, Ellington, Basie, Marsalis, and Bearden have in common? Me. [Laughter.]

Edwards: I know! It's interesting. I guess we can talk about some of them individually. I guess I'm most curious about your relationship with Ralph Ellison. How many years older was he?

Murray: Two. I'm seventy-eight, and he died at eighty. He was two years ahead of me at school. May have been more than that, but he had been there two years when I got there—Tuskegee. So we were contemporaries. I was there looking for—you know, it's like in *South to a Very Old Place:* "I'm the one determines what the value is." I would say, "Well, this is a pretty good book to read." I was doing that with upperclassmen. "This guy ain't shit. This guy is pretty good. This guy is a hustler." I was making all those judgments. But I think they stand up. I was looking for people who were serious about all this stuff, about the ancestral imperatives. Who was really shucking and who was doing the other stuff. I was looking. And he [Ellison] impressed me more than any other upperclassman. Some other guys, they looked good, they dressed well. They were taking Mr. Sprague's course in the novel. They were reading all these novels. *Clarissa Harlowe, Tom Jones.* Ellison and all these guys were reading these books. So I watched this stuff happening, and I noticed Ralph doing some other stuff. I knew he was trying to sculpt. I noticed that he would be at the other end of the library with his music paper spread out, doing copy work. And he was in the band, so he wasn't a cadet. I was a cadet. You had to be a cadet at Tuskegee. ROTC. It was like a Big Ten school, like a farm and technical school. See, Booker T. Washington wanted *everything*. [Laughter.]

Edwards: Which is not what you usually hear. The concept in [my] mind is something else. Something more limited.

Murray: Right. We had the damndest library. So the two hardest guys to read, black writers, because of all the literary background and references, are Ellison and Murray. All the other guys from Howard . . . you can read Sterling Brown and all these guys easily. But so far as the kinds of references you have to know: Ellison and Murray.

So I was watching Ralph. And then I was reading these books, and I would see his name in the books. They had that little slip in the books when you used to borrow them from the library. There was a place where you had to sign for it, and then they would stamp it. When you checked out a book, you could open the back of the book, and you could see the last time it was read and who had read it. Then I got to know his signature, and he was reading the books I was going to read; he had read them. So that was a real upper-classman for you. But he was always a loner-type guy, watchful-eyed, so I didn't venture to introduce myself to him. He worked in the library, a part-time student job.

The first exchange we ever had was . . . I had read Sinclair Lewis's *Arrow-smith* in a Modern Library edition, which was a flexible edition at that time. A green suede binding. I had read André Maurois's book *Ariel: The Life of Shelley.* I was reading about Byron, Shelley, and Keats and what those guys were reading. I was reading about reading and all that. I was a real college student. Everybody figured I should have gone to Yale or Harvard—to Brown, to an Ivy League school. But I was going to Tuskegee, and I was not going to let anybody at Harvard, Yale, and whatnot get a better education than was available to me there. So I was reading these books and what these guys were doing. And they'd talk about how Shelley would be reading all the time. He would fold the book and stick it in his pocket, his back pocket. So I had a flexible book, Sinclair Lewis's *Arrowsmith,* and I'd fold it up and stick it in my pocket, wherever I stopped reading. I wouldn't put a bookmark in it. Just fold it and stick it in my hip pocket, like Shelley. I was probably wearing a tam and a goatee too at that time. *Benvenuto Cellini.* I probably

had seen that movie with Fredric March or something like that. All this bohe-
mian stuff that was part of being collegiate, if you were serious. So I go to
the library to turn this book in or to get it renewed, and Ralph is at the desk.
And Ralph looks at the book and says, "What do you think this is? A pocket
edition?" [Laughter.] That's the first exchange.

But I would see him, and I would notice him, and I would see books. . . .
When I went to read T. S. Eliot, his name was there. When I went to read
Robinson Jeffers, all those things, his name was in there. In many of the
books, he was the only guy. Then Hamilton and I were reading different
books.

But I really didn't meet Ralph until about 1942. I knew he was in New
York. I knew he had started writing. He had majored in music, but it didn't
surprise me that he was writing reviews in magazines, because I knew he was
a great reader and he was one of the favorites of Mr. Sprague's, who was my
English teacher, too. We used to talk about Ralph. I was reading all of the
magazines. I'd pick up one and say, "Hey, this guy reviewed a book by
Waters Turpin called *These Low Grounds.*" I can remember this. "Oh, I saw
that phrase that Ellison said the other day, 'Malraux pointed out the other day
that we are returning to fundamentals.' " I'd say, "Damn, boy! He's up
there!" He was into the life. So when I came to New York in '42, another
Tuskegian named Mike Rabb was up here on a fellowship going to Columbia,
taking hospital administration because he was being moved into the position
of administrative director of the Tuskegee Institute Hospital. He was staying
over here at the Y. He and I were talking about other Tuskegians who were
staying in New York, and he mentioned Ellison, whom he had known. He
had a nickname for Ellison. He always referred to Ellison as Sousa, as in
John Philip, because he was the student concert master. If you'd see the band
in the stands, Ellison would be the guy conducting it. So Mike called him
Sousa. So we went to see Ralph. He was living right up on the hill there
where CCNY was. He was married to a nightclub singer named Rose Poin-
dexter. When we walked into his place, the first thing I saw when he sat back
in his chair, the first thing I saw was the Malraux over his shoulder. Then,
having been introduced to him, I kept in touch with him on my own. It didn't
take him long to find out that I was one of the few guys who read the same
kinds of books. So it was automatic. Like that.

Edwards: So the two of you had a relationship from then on?

Murray: Mmm hmm. We were writing letters and so forth. You know
about the stuff that I read at the funeral, the memorial?

Edwards: Yes. I was there. They're wonderful letters.

Murray: There's a whole collection of those things, which I'll show you one day.

That was '42. In '48 or '47, after I got converted to the reserves from the Air Force at the end of the war, I came to NYU to go to graduate school. And Ralph was by this time out of the merchant marines and into *Invisible Man.* I got back in touch with him. That fall when I came to grad school at NYU, he had published the first excerpt, the prologue from *Invisible Man,* in *Horizon* magazine. Then *Partisan* bought [the] "Battle Royal" [section]. But meanwhile we were in touch, you see, and I'd come up to see him. This is during the [cultural] heyday of 52nd Street.

Edwards: Right. So you're busy. [Laughter.]

Murray: You know, catching Duke at the Paramount, catching those [Broadway matinee] shows. But my hangout was the 42nd Street Library, because graduate school was at night at NYU at that time. So Ralph was working on *Invisible Man* across the street from Rockefeller Center, across 49th Street, right across from Saks. Eight floors up there was a jewelry store that was run by some friends of Francis Steegmuller, author of *Flaubert and Madame Bovary* and *Maupassant: A Lion in the Path.* In the back of the jewelry store there was an office which they didn't use. Francis had used it, but he was in Europe at that time. So Ralph would get up in the morning and pack his attaché case, dress up, and go to work. Sometimes he would come down to the library and we would talk. Or we would stop at Gotham Book Mart.

Edwards: Were you writing at this time?

Murray: Yeah, I was trying to. But I was reading and figuring out what I was going to do. I had tried to write plays and stuff like that. By this time I was into Mann, Hemingway, and all that. Because it was out of Mann, out of Thomas Mann, that I got the idea that you could find a basis, an aesthetic model in your [own] musical idiom for literature. So when he started talking about dialectic orchestration and leitmotifs and things like that, I started thinking about riffs, breaks, and things like that. And then as I started studying, it all made for *The Hero and the Blues*—more for *The Hero and the Blues* than for *Stomping the Blues.* In *Stomping the Blues,* I just go back and clarify the whole notion of organizing literature around musical composition. If I could find the literary equivalent of Ellington, I could one up on Melville, Twain, and Whitman.

Edwards: What do you see as the relationship between your work and Ellison's? *Is* there a relationship? There's certainly not, I don't think, a *simple* relationship.

Murray: Well, they're two different things. His is more—well, the political implications are more obvious. Whereas my aesthetic preoccupation and my sense of the total human context—although I work as hard as I can to get the local color and idiomatic particulars right, but that to me is what the writer always does. But you want the political, the social to seem incidental. You get that, and you don't even know you've got it. So he's more—I've been thinking about that. I was thinking about the differences in the sensibility. There's a certain amount of explanation of black folk stuff for white folks, which I refuse to do. See, he would do that. He would say certain things which I wouldn't say.

Edwards: Because of your different sensibility.

Murray: Yeah. It's just that you take it all, and you do it. See, you do it, and it's like "C-Jam Blues." You know, you swing it. And that's it. And then the guy himself says, "Geez, I wish I was brown-skinned." That's what you try to do.

My work doesn't ever stick to ethnicity and yet I don't want anyone ever to be thought of as a greater authority on ethnicity. They should say, "Ask him, he *knows*." Or, "He's got the voice. He's got the this, he's got the that." But the whole thing is—like Duke, you see . . . I want to say that Negroes never looked or sounded better than in Murray and Duke. With everybody else, they've got to go through a certain amount of mud. But they sump'm else, Murray and Duke. That's an *ambition.* You see what I'm saying? So the guy says, "I wanna be like that." See, I don't have any problem with teaching at an exclusive school, a white school, like Washington and Lee. When all the kids run after me it's because they're my boys. "I wanna be like him." It's that type of thing that you want to do. And you want to cut across that. Why is Stan Getz playing like that? Why are those guys running around looking like Miles? What's Gerry Mulligan *doing?* Every time he picks up his horn he wants you to feel that he was in Kansas City. He was hanging out with that. He wants to say, "I have as much authority dealing with these nuances as these guys. I don't want you to say that mine is different. I don't want you to say that I'm playing with an accent." Like the guy says, "Don't bother Stan Kenton, he thinks he's swinging." [Laughter.]

So the difference between me and Ralph Ellison is the difference between emphasis and the difference in literary strategy. But we have much of the same information and there's no conflict at all in our ultimate goals. But I could not write *Invisible Man*. Look, look, with all the stuff and all the talk and so forth, Invisible Man is a victim. He's got the possibilities, but he's in a *hole*.

Edwards: But he doesn't submit. He's ultimately committed to the struggle of life.

Murray: He's a tragic hero with the possibility of redemption. Not really redemption, but rejuvenation, metamorphosis, all those things. But basically all the stuff that's happening to him is closer to a sense of tragedy.

Edwards: But a universal sense of tragedy.

Murray: Of course. We're not talking about disaster. We're talking about the nobility of tragedy. I'm interested in epics. It's another literary strategy altogether. I write about heroic possibility. I'm one of the few Americans to write about heroism. If you take me somewhere and the guy says, "We gotta get together because we gon' do this and them people did this to us and they did that to us, so we mad as hell," I'm going to say, "We gon' get up in the morning and we gon' do this and we gon' do that, and then we gon' *zap* the motherfuckers!" You see, that's the difference, and that's what they're not ready for. They're wallowing around being victims. I can't *stand* that! Because there is none of that in jazz. You triumph over that.

Edwards: Stomp it.

Murray: You see what I mean? And all those people know that. They go home. They play some low-down dirty blues. What did they want to do? Go out and fight white people, or get into bed with somebody? They don't want to go out there and talk about no damn injustice and taxes and no money. The only time they talk about money [in blues songs] is when they don't have enough money to hold a gal, so she went off with another guy. So they're talking about art as fertility ritual.

Edwards: Which is what the blues is about.

Murray: You stomp the blues—that's a purification ritual. Why do you purify it? You have these two universal rituals—one to purify the environment of that which menaces human life, the other is the fertility ritual to ensure the continuation of the species. To revitalize existence. The union of lovers ensures the continuation of life. That's why we have the copulating blues. *So I can get in her pants.* [Laughter.] *If I don't get in her pants, ain't gon' be*

no tomorrow—for me or nobody else! We got all these children out of wedlock because we will stomp the blues every Saturday night. This goes back
not only to Storyville but also to Sophocles. Dionysus, man.

And I keep hoping against hope that I'm gonna win, you know, that people
will see that our foreparents had respect for themselves, that they believed in
their own humanity and integrity. They could not be torn apart. They weren't
putting on a front. They were for real. In *Gone with the Wind,* when Mammy
is fitting Scarlett O'Hara's corset and she tells her mistress, "You done had a
baby, you ain't never gon' be no eighteen-and-a-half inches again," it's because Mammy knows what is behind the façade of the plantation mistress.
She made Scarlett into a lady. Our foreparents knew what was behind the
myth of whiteness, because they helped create it. Later, Scarlett O'Hara sees
the devastation of the South, and still she keeps her dignity. Who taught her
that? Aunt Jemima. Uncle Ben.

Edwards: Let's talk a little bit about Romare Bearden.
Murray: Yeah, Romy.

Edwards: And your relationship to him.
Murray: I had known about Bearden on my own, but I also knew of
Bearden's work through Ralph. In fact, in [my daughter's] room there's a
painting which Bearden originally gave to Ralph. Ralph gave it to me because
he ran out of space, and then I was instrumental in his getting a *bigger*
Bearden painting when I got him to do [his essay] on Bearden for the Albany
exhibition. Then he was supposed to do another and he copped out on it and
I had to do it. But by this time I was Bearden's chief literary advisor, so to
speak. We [Bearden and I] collaborated on most of his stuff.

Edwards: When you say collaborate, what do you mean?
Murray: Frames of reference and titles. He'd say, "Well, *we're* gonna do
a one-man show." And then I'd say, "We oughta do something on jazz."
And Bearden would say, "What should I do?" Now, we spent more time
with each other than either of us spent with any other guys. Looking at paintings together, going to exhibitions. Doing things like that. So we could talk
painting. We could talk music.

I met him in Paris in 1950. . . . Then, when I retired, we became buddies.
We saw each other on an even more regular basis than Ellison and I did,
although Ellison and I talked on the phone a lot. Romy and I would get
together and we would go and look at all these paintings. That would have
started in 1963, when I moved to New York and got back in touch with him.

We were always doing things together—looking at paintings, buying books.
And when he started making a lot of money with his painting, he would buy
books. He would buy two of them, you know. And we used to meet at
Books & Company, because a friend of ours had started it. We would meet
over there every Saturday and we would hold court. People would find us
over there. Meanwhile, I'd be setting up the outline and naming the paintings.
He would say, "What should I do now?" You know contemporary painting,
the major painters, right?

Edwards: Sure.

Murray: See, Romy can't stand up without Pieter de Hooch, Vermeer, the
Dutch on this side—he [even] looked like a Dutchman—and Matisse on the
other. To get to modern art, you can't go back through [the] Middle Passage
and get there that way. Because they don't get into modern art. You go
through the Musee de L'Homme. Romy and I would communicate just like
that. All painting concepts and stuff like that. So he'd say, "What can I do
next?" And so I'd say, "What about a Storyville Odalisque?" You know,
Matisse. Bing! He's off. You know, he might do twelve variations on that. So
what has he got? You can see it right off. You can see the design. I would
think in terms of design, but also in poetic and metaphorical terms. So I
would say, "Well, you've got a professor." See, the piano player. "You got
an ornate mirror. You got a room. You've got a woman partly dressed. This
guy sitting over here." So you've got the Mandrian-like stylization of the
keys. Overall, it's like Matisse's odalisques. You know, they're very busy. A
long way from the cut-outs. It's boogie-woogie. It comes right out of pointil-
lism. So you can give these things the illusion of busyness.

All these are visual statements with literary overtones. So that, as abstract
as the paintings were, they come back with a representational type of thing.
But what saved it, how *we,* in a sense, saved it, was—he was moving in a
direction to make it known—I came up with the concept of "The Prevalence
of Ritual." He was doing a bunch of conjure women, playing around with
that. This was when I came on board of collaboration. We were doing lots of
other things, but then I started visiting his studio a lot, and he liked my
phrases. And he was a big reader of mine. All you've got to do is look at the
paintings and see how many trains there are. Trains! I saw these conjure
women. And there was a bestseller a few years before that was called *The
Prevalence of Witches,* and that phrase stuck with me. I gave it to him, and
mine stuck—"The Prevalence of Ritual." Wham! It hit him. And that, I

submit, saved his painting from genre painting. You know what I mean by that?

If you look at a painter like Jacob Lawrence, his painting is genre—what Negroes look like, how they live, the way their neighborhood looks. These are the peasants represented as art, like the wonderful peasant life of France. Painting critics call that genre.

Edwards: So how did "The Prevalence of Ritual" elevate or save Bearden from genre?

Murray: The stylization overshadows the report. So Romy could do a series on anything and it wouldn't be genre. See all of this jazz we did? Well, it's not just illustrating jazz. [Murray is pointing to a large Romare Bearden painting hanging in the apartment.] That's just a painting on its own right. See, that's Duke Ellington. Look at that painting. Look at the variation. Look at these rectangles; they're different colors. Look at these rectangles on the piano legs. Look at this! Look at the glistening on the top of the piano. That's a half-moon. So you see how these figures are in there. Look how the white is played with. Now, instead of the keyboard, it's that little fence between the ringside and the others. But you've still got the same type of strokes in the painting.

Edwards: So it's the stylization—

Murray: It's swinging! That sonofabitch is *swinging,* man. But if you just get the report. . . . This is not quirky twist on a report; that's another thing. But it's the *painting* that does it. Art is a process by which raw experience is stylized into aesthetic statement. So what we have on the wall is not a report, but an aesthetic statement. When you deal with those fundamentals like that, you can keep it in focus. You can learn to appreciate what the guy's doing. You can see how he's playing with these things. This becomes not white but *light.* So the drumheads are light. They're reflecting light. So, too, with the shine on Duke's knee.

Edwards: What's this painting called?

Murray: *Duke Ellington on Stage.* Oh, I named a lot of them, and I set the context for a lot of them. Romy would call my wife and say, "Well, I've been pretty busy. Tell Al, tell Al I got to see him. I've got all these orphans over here that need names." [Laughter.] There was no sense of competition. Bearden loved writing and I loved painting. We had extremely close and shared aesthetic insights.

Edwards: You've written books and essays about music and literature. Do you think you'll ever write a book about art?

Murray: Not really. You know the Bearden piece? That's about it.

Edwards: You obviously have a lot to offer on the subject.

Murray: I might. You never know what'll happen. . . . Little articles might just happen if I find I want to say this, want to say that. Just like you want to come by and talk to me about something—

Edwards: Might stimulate something?

Murray: Mmm hmm.

The Soloist: Albert Murray's Blues People

Joe Wood / 1996

From *VLS*, no. 142 (February 1996), pp. 17–22. Reprinted by permission of the author and *The Village Voice*.

Lesson 1: *Albert Murray is not famous.*

Murray has long argued his opinions with the ferocity of a dragon fighter, ever since the publication of his first book, *The Omni-Americans,* in 1970. Back then he was trying to outpoint the youthful black Barakas of the day, trying to peel away the long shadow of his friend Ralph Ellison, trying to find his own voice for fiction at age 54. Twenty-five years later there is a shelf of accolades: a National Book Award nomination, a membership in the Century Club, publication of one of his titles in the Modern Library series. And yet Murray remains something of an unknown. He is an unattended teacher, the last of an endangered breed of literary-political thinkers.

The hope for a change in the weather is minimal. Except: National fascination with well-read black people (see "black public intellectuals") is at a postmodern high, perhaps commensurate with the equally popular notion of black intellectual inferiority (see Charles Murray). Except: Interest in black conservatism, that species of political behavior often lauded as *honest* for its unflattering descriptions of black folk, is also selling like hotcakes. Except: If Stanley Crouch is the mind of Wynton Marsalis, as one writer recently put it, Murray is the mind of the mind of Wynton. When Lincoln Center recently decided to give the jazz program Crouch and Marsalis run equal standing with its European classical side, the Center bowed to one of Murray's lifelong projects. "The objective was to be a part of that . . . ," he has said. "Once I'm at Lincoln Center, [the place] is different. [The objective] is not to be *like* them. It's to make Lincoln Center like *I* think it should be."

Lesson 2: The Omni-Americans *is his motherlode.*

One of my favorite professors used to say that most intellectuals have one idea, which they struggle with all their lives. If they succeed in expressing it well once, they are very lucky. What this luck usually amounts to, the teacher said, is one good film, one good book of essays, one good novel. In Murray's case, that book would be *The Omni-Americans,* in which he argues that blues, like all fine aesthetic idioms, tells universal tales.

Omni is a book about American literature. It borrows heavily from the work of other thinkers. From historian Constance Rourke's *American Humor,* in which the author argues that *"homo Americanus"* is made of one part entrepreneurial Yankee, one part frontiersman/Indian, and one part Negro, comes the title conception: Murray's "omni-American" is the product of a rich "mulatto culture" which has given as much to black people as blacks have given to it. "It is all too true that Negroes unlike the Yankee and the backwoodsman were slaves whose legal status was that of property," he writes in *Omni.* "But it is also true—and as things have turned out, even more significant—that they were slaves who were living in the presence of more human freedom and individual opportunity than they or anybody else had ever seen before. That the conception of being a free man in America was infinitely richer than any notion of individuality in the Africa of that period goes without saying."

Murray also relies on Kenneth Burke's distinction between frames of rejection and acceptance. "Out of the frame of rejection, you get the plaint, the elegy, the complaint, you get moral outcry, you get protest, you get the idea of victim," he told me when I saw him recently. "That's because you're rejecting the human condition. The other frame that we've talked about is a frame of acceptance. Not the acceptance of injustice, inequality, or any of those things like that. But acceptance of the fact that life is a struggle." Murray singles out Frederick Douglass and Harriet Tubman as particularly obvious paradigms of this type of acceptance, and says they represent true American heroism.

The writer's interest in heroism bears the stamp of his favorite literary figures, all stalwart modernists: W. H. Auden, James Joyce, T. S. Eliot, Ernest Hemingway, André Malraux, Thomas Mann. What he likes is their focus on the predicament of the individual human being, the struggle to face the worries of existence, and to negotiate a place among other people. "So that's where the blues comes in," he explained. "Where we get my thing in is to say the blues is an aesthetic device for confrontation and improvisation."

Of course, he had put it plainly enough before:

[In the blues] there is, for instance, the seemingly inherent emphasis on rugged individual endurance. There is also the candid acknowledgement and sober acceptance of adversity as an inescapable condition of human existence—and per-

haps in consequence an affirmative disposition toward all obstacles, whether
urban or rural, whether political or metaphysical. . . . But perhaps above all else
the blues-oriented hero image represents the American embodiment of the man
whose concept of being able to live happily ever afterwards is most consistent
with the moral of all dragon-encounters: *Improvisation is the ultimate human
(i.e., heroic) endowment.*

This improvisation in the face of what Murray calls "antagonistic cooperation" from the challenges of human existence is dialectical, but not in a
Marxist sense. Good writers present heroes who struggle with dragons and
blue devils honorably using all the swords and other weapons at hand. In the
process, such writers create two kinds of examples. Their "representative
anecdotes" show the best ways to struggle with life's chaos, and the writer's
own improvisations demonstrate the fact, and beauty, of human possibility.

Lesson 3: *Albert Murray likes to teach.*

I began our conversation by complaining that his man Marsalis sounds
more like a curator than a musician. I wondered when Wynton will take the
musics he grew up with and transform them in the way that people used to
transform Cole Porter songs.

"I see what you mean," he said. His face tightened like a young surgeon's
hand. "But it's a bigger problem for Wynton to do it, simply because he
knows more [than funk musicians]. If you operate on the level of convention,
James Brown and those guys are not responding to as much music. What
complicates the quest is what Harold Rosenberg called 'the tradition of the
new.' I think a number of the commentators have backed into the tradition of
the new. Anybody who thinks that innovation is the prime imperative for the
creative person does not know anything about art or the history of art. Because that is pursuit of novelty. Nothing could be more superficial or ephem-
eral," he said, laughing from his chest.

Lesson 4: *Albert Murray thinks jazz can save American lives.*

Murray says the blues idiom's encouragement of confrontation and improvisation helps the nation survive. According to him, jazz artists have "synthesize[d] all the [American] forces as nobody else has done," largely because
black people's cultural slate was wiped clean when they arrived on these
shores. The idiom they developed gave them a special responsibility. "Today,
America's only possible hope is that the Negroes might save us, which is all
we're trying to do," Murray recently told the *New Yorker.* "We've got Louis,

Duke, Count, and Ralph [Ellison], and now we're trying to do it with Wynton and Stanley. That's all we are—just a bunch of Negroes *trying* to save America."

Lesson 5: *Albert Murray takes his individualism seriously.*

How different from the solitude of writing literature jazz seems, now that the music has come to signify the respectful conversation of a team, each player gracefully enabling the improvisations of another. But the striking thing about Murray's passion for good literature and music is how similarly he sees these art forms. To him, both are essentially heroic idioms. When he does discuss artistic collaboration, Murray mostly means engaging the masterworks. "Creative effort means entering a dialogue with the form," he told me. "Each new effective aesthetic statement alters the existing emotional scale. So it's not simply a dialogue, it's a colloquy."

It is a tenet of the modernism ethos—in literature as in music, the artist should know and refer to the work of dead masters, and with the few who are alive today. To Murray, a good artist fashions gold out of the ore of folk art—songs, pop writing, television, movies—and ordinary experience. His fine art must finally respond, however, to other people's best art.

But and but: what comes through after a session of close listening to the man's work—even on jazz—is not an interest in collaboration as an end, but as a means for the individual player. Heroic self-expression is what counts. Louis Armstrong, Murray suggests in the latest book of essays, "was not unaware of the fact that he was in effect a culture hero (not unlike, say, Prometheus), the bringer of indispensable, existential equipment for the survival of humanity." Count Basie, an accompanist par excellence, worked other musicians like a quiet god:

> Sometimes the accompanist, for all his unobtrusiveness, actually leads and prompts the soloist. Sometimes he only follows, perhaps most often as if he were whispering yes, yes, yes; and then, and then, and then; go on, go on, go on; amen, so be it. Even when he engages in call and response exchanges, it is always as if the soloist is carying on a dialogue with someone who is either absent or totally imaginary. But always the accompanist is there to keep the melodic line and its frame of reference intact and the soloist in key, in tune, and in time.

There was also Duke, whose place in the national pantheon was "not a matter of election campaigns. You must earn your own way in as gods and heroes have always had to do, through the intrinsic merit of what you do and how you do it, and as a result of the undeniability, the depth and scope, and the durability of its impact. And, of course, that is exactly what Duke Ellington had done."

Their godliness, Murray says, makes these musicians very similar to their literary cousins. While he admires the scholarship—the ability to converse with tradition—men like Thomas Mann and Ernest Hemingway bring to their work, he finally loves them for being able to improvise a singular synthesis of all they know, with courage. In doing so, and in producing art which reflects these values, such artists demonstrate humanity's best attributes. He elaborates in the middle of an essay on Ellington in his latest book of nonfiction, *The Blue Devils of Nada*:

> No one can seriously accuse the Hemingway hero of not using his head. With the exception of Harry Morgan, the typical Hemingway hero is almost always not only a thinking man but also a reading man and frequently a writing man. He does not indulge in academic abstractions and intellectualized clichés and slogans but neither does he rely on tribal instinct, superstition, magic, or hand me down rules of thumb. He proceeds on concrete information, his discipline being that of an empiricist who responds in terms of what he personally knows and feels rather than what somebody else has decided he would know and feel. . . . Robert Penn Warren once wrote that the Hemingway hero was becoming aware of nada. Perhaps one might add that he is someone who has the blues (is bedeviled by blue devils) because, like Ecclesiastes, he has confronted the absurdity of human existence and knows that each moment and each experience count.

This passage can only be read as Murray's conception of the ideal temperament of the literary artist. Murray's "auteur" conception sticks to the mainstream modernist concern about the individuality of any artist, whether musical or literary.

But and but and but: Murray neglects the artist's need to collaborate with her audience. One suspects the process is more obvious in the case of jazz performers than writers. No matter how much chaos they face down, musicians have never been inattentive to their audiences—or they couldn't play in public for very long. Murray himself points out that Ellington worked many crowds—he wrote music for films, dance halls, opera houses—with integrity but with flexibility. But he doesn't see that this makes Duke an artist collaborating with other artists collaborating with listeners. Not only does Murray's

emphasis on individual heroism distort the first kind of collaboration, it neglects the second.

Lesson 6: *Albert Murray doesn't believe in a "black audience."*

The extent of the collaboration between writers of fiction and their readers
is a matter best taken up by academicians. But at the end of the day the fact
of that collaboration is undeniable, if only because writers must use a shared
tongue. Sometimes sharing causes fights. For the black writer especially the
audience can be a difficult partner. Two of her audiences—the blacks and the
whites—share a tongue but are at odds. Nobody has written about the difficulty this creates for the black writer as well as James Weldon Johnson did
in his 1938 essay, "The Dilemma of the Negro Author."

> The moment a Negro writer takes up his pen or sits down to his typewriter he
> is immediately called upon to solve, consciously and unconsciously, the prob-
> lem of the double audience. To whom shall he address himself, to his own black
> group or to white America? Many a Negro writer has fallen down, as it were,
> between these two stools.

Today's landscape is more complicated than the one Johnson describes.
Numbers of Latino and Asian readers have increased since the time when
Johnson wrote, and racial attitudes among all readers have changed consider-
ably. Also, many black writers write in part to traditions and audiences that
are not European or American: There is Gabriel García Márquez in Toni
Morrison's writing and Chinua Achebe, too. Yet, Johnson's dilemma is still
as real as the chasmic split over the O. J. verdict.

Johnson goes on to explain the conflicting expectations of the two audiences, which amount to a white demand for stencils of docile or savage Negroes, and a black demand for respectable and "nice" Negroes. The way out
is not easy:

> I judge there is not a single Negro writer who is not, at least secondarily, im-
> pelled by the desire to make his work have some effect on the white world for
> the good of his race. It may be thought that the work of the Negro writer, on
> account of this last named condition, gains in pointedness what it loses in
> breadth. Be that as it may, the situation is for the time one in which he is
> inextricably placed. Of course, the Negro author can try the experiment of put-
> ting black America in the orchestra chairs, so to speak, and keeping white

America in the gallery, but he is likely at any moment to find his audience
shifting places on him, and sometimes without notice.

Murray's answer is to insist on the essential sameness of all Americans.
Since Negroes are part of America, Negro expression can't help but keep in
mind (and heart and body) Americanness; Du Bois's veil of "double consciousness" doesn't exist. For Murray, Louis Armstrong's music "is if anything even more representative of American affirmation and promise in the
face of adversity than the festive reiterations of the most elaborate display of
any Fourth of July fireworks. . . . Indeed, during the year following World
War II the sound of Ambassador Satchmo came to have more worldwide
appeal than the image of Yankee Doodle Dandy ever did, not to mention the
poster image of Uncle Sam. . . ." And whites are no less culturally mulatto
than the Ambassador. In one essay Murray quotes a friend's approving remarks about Hemingway's attention to the truth. "For Ellison, everything
Hemingway wrote 'was imbued with a spirit beyond the tragic with which I
could feel at home, for it was close to the feeling of the blues, which are,
perhaps, as close as Americans can come to expressing the spirit of
tragedy.' "
    Implicit is this idea: When you're addressing the American audience, a
mulatto audience, you're talking to everybody without regard to race. This
saves America—it tells the entire nation of the facts about itself, and reminds
it of its ideals in a nonpartisan fashion.
    Except there's a hidden set of concerns. When Johnson concludes—

The making of a common audience out of white and black America presents
the Negro author with enough difficulties to constitute a third horn of his dilemma. It is a task that is a very high test for all his skill and abilities, but it can
be and has been accomplished. The equipped Negro author working at his best
in his best known material can achieve this end; but standing on his racial
foundation, he must fashion something that rises above race, and reaches out to
the universal in truth and beauty. And so, when a Negro author does write so as
to fuse white and black America into one interested and approving audience he
has performed no slight feat, and has most likely done a sound piece of literary
work.

—he sounds like Murray, or vice versa, but the difference between the two
men is substantial. While Johnson acknowledges the dilemma in the first
place, Murray is evasive. He contends the color line doesn't matter, yet he

always keeps it in mind. "I have more white guys and gals reading my books than colored guys simply because they read more books," he told me. "You're not hoping to reach but so many Afro-Americans or whatever it is they call themselves today. You're not going to reach them because they don't read books. They certainly don't read books that have the ambition to be on the same level as Kenneth Burke or Malraux." Like his books, for example.

I thought: surely a mulatto culture implies a heterogeneous audience—even if that audience is at war with itself.

Lesson 7: *Albert Murray likes his "representative anecdotes" to reflect "ancestral imperatives."*

"Even if it's a 900-page novel, it's an anecdote. All of Proust is an anecdote of turn-of-the-century France. . . . The Hemingway section [of *The Blue Devils of Nada*] keeps it as simple as I think I can make it, which is, you write about what you know about. Try to get how you really feel about it. If your sensibility is comprehensive enough and your craft is good enough, then what you come out with is probably a representative anecdote." He used Richard Wright's *Native Son* as an example of a book that is not a representative anecdote. "What is missing in [Bigger] Thomas was that he was not a representative character. And yet people interpreted the book [this way]: 'This tells me what it's like to be a Negro in America.' "

I wondered whether he could see what I meant *this* time. Mostly I listened like a good young man. I should have said: Surely black people knew that Bigger isn't representative of all black people, even if the characterization was off. To whom, in Murray's eyes, was Wright *misrepresenting* black people? Those misled "people" simply have to be *white,* which concedes Johnson's point without conceding it: Murray knows the two American audiences bring very different sensibilities to their reading chairs.

I asked Murray whether he thought Jake Barnes, the protagonist in Hemingway's *The Sun Also Rises,* is representative of any community. The "white" community for example.

"[Hemingway] was writing about the predicament of man. So that's the challenge. Do these guys identify with Scooter [the protagonist in Murray's novels] or do they receive it as news as to what it's like to be a black boy in America? And yet I wanted authentically—you get all the local color, all of the specifics are there. [The protagonist] doesn't have to be a character with no specific cultural affiliation. The problem of the artist is to take these idiomatic particulars and process them in a way that gives them universal impact."

But that's a big burden, I said. I should have said: Why does a writer have any responsibility to authentically "represent" people who don't read her?

He explained that the representative anecdote should reflect the "ancestral imperatives"—God, I would have thought he was making this up as he went along, except I'd seen the idea in his books. The ancestral imperatives are various, but the best ones enable a people to survive; blues confrontation and improvisation fit the bill. Only people like Richard Wright didn't get it. "This guy can't swing. You wouldn't have thought he was within 10,000 miles of Earl Hines, and the Grand Terrace."

So now I wanted to know whether the blues-oriented Hemingway shared ancestral imperatives with black people. Were their imperatives the same?

"I don't know whether I'm interested in that or not," he said. He couldn't see himself having the same ancestral imperatives as the son of a doctor from the Midwest, but he did share a dialogue with the very literary masters Hemingway engaged. And these writers are white. "You can't have a dialogue with a form that does not exist. If you're going to be a writer, and you want to be a good writer, and you're writing novels, you're either going to be an American novelist, a French novelist, or a German novelist. You're not going to be an African novelist, because they don't write. Shit, you can't do that."

"But," I said, "you can have a dialogue with your audiences." Any good writer—Africans included—wants to and does speak to living souls, not just Flaubert and Hemingway. Or even Soyinka. He might want to speak to particular African audiences.

Murray's voice rose. "But that's not what your audience is. Can't you understand? I'm talking about being a writer. Just like a guy talking about being a movie actor. That's not the same as dancing in front of a chief. You say, 'Well that's performing, too.' But that's crap. Anybody who can't see the difference between a movie star and a slave dancing in a mudhole. . . ."

I listened obediently to the man who suddenly seemed elderly, his age. He couldn't hear all that well, his back kept him hobbled. He was at the mercy of young doctors and he was running out of time. I remembered the last sentence of a recent newspaper interview he'd done: "the most radical thing that you can do," he'd told the Boston journalist, "is to be a nice-looking, brown-skinned American guy, well-dressed, well-educated; that's the most dangerous sonofabitch in the country!" I got the point: he really is interested in having some effect on the white reader for the good of the race. *He wants us to be respectable.*

Lesson 8: *Albert Murray slams the lid on black protest literature.*

I remind you that his big idea is that blues voices laugh in the face of the oppressive or just plain entropic forces, and that writers should write characters who live despite the chaos, and without complaining too much. He told me:

> You confront the fact that life is a low down dirty shame. Anybody who can see the natural history of Negroes in the United States can see that. You wake up in the morning and you're a slave, you're not going to kid yourself. It's unjust. Some guy will just complain about it and moan about it. Another guy will listen around and whatnot and find out about the Underground Railroad. So he accepts the fact that he's a slave as a necessity for struggle. That qualifies him as being a part of the heroic or epical mode. You see, because he can extend from one to many, that is, he's an example. That's why he's a hero. He inspires other people to accept that.

Murray never goes so far as to suggest that anybody ignore the dragons of racism, but he is very impatient with art that spends a lot of time talking about them. "American protest fiction . . . concerns itself not with the ambiguities of self-improvement and self-extension, not with the evaluation of the individual as protagonist, but rather with representing a world of collective victims whose survival and betterment depend not upon self-determination but upon a change of heart in their antagonists, who thereupon will cease being villains and become patrons of social welfare!" Murray is careful not to condemn propagandistic art in general; elements of propaganda, he concedes, appear in all literature. "Nevertheless, there are many reasons why it is all but impossible for a serious writer of fiction to engage his craft as such in a political cause, no matter how worthy, without violating his very special integrity as an artist in some serious way."

A few pages later he goes even further:

> Writers have always thrived on oppression, poverty, alienation and the like. Feodor Dostoevski, for example, was very poor, much oppressed. . . . He was imprisoned; and one time he came within minutes of being officially lynched. But he wrote good books. Because he liked good books. . . . But the sad fact is that there is very little to show that very many U.S. Negro writers have ever actually tried to write major novels.

Major novelists, then, do not complain about racism. White folks—the only audience Murray imagines—don't need to hear those complaints because all they do is tell the dragon he has power over black life. Would-be major novelists, he contends, ought to enter the complex lives of their characters, which in the case of Negroes are always circumscribed but rarely defined by racism.

The last point is brilliant. There is a certain formula to black lamentation, and a good writer can master it in a very short time. Until the recent change in climate, such lamentation seemed to be the kind of black writing preferred by liberal whites. Now the rage is for stories by and about well-adjusted and responsible black people. As with the older predigested formulation, good writers can run the current line with their eyes closed—but good writing forces an encounter with the demands of those often conflicting white and black audiences. If the writer displeases too many blacks, she loses fellow strugglers on her side of the great divide. If she displeases too many whites, she may find herself unable to publish at all.

The serious writer simply can't help conversing with the world around her. In this way her fiction is collaborative. If she is hip to the spirit of the age, if she is writing in America, if her characters are black, if their lives are affected by the forces that help shape the lives of most black Americans, if she is aware of the complex moral and existential issues facing them, she will write damning words about white supremacy. Murray's well-dressed black man knows that, but he may not realize this: If the novelist chooses not to make any of her characters heroic, even tragically heroic, she can be sure that some critics will dismiss the book as lacking in subtlety. They will say she is too *angry*. That she protests too much. Others will suggest that she is insufficiently angry or that she does not love her people enough. And she might answer with that old perfect riddle: *I listened to what the characters had to say*. Only her serious readers (women, men, black, white, brown, yellow, American, global) will get the joke.

Lesson 9: *Albert Murray dons his uniform.*

Murray's distaste for black "protest fiction" has roots outside of literary modernism. While his embrace of edifying heroism also resembles W. E. B. Du Bois's Talented Tenth formulation, it more directly stems from the mind of Booker T. Washington. In *Up From Slavery,* the founder of Tuskegee shows the philosophy he peddled to students like Murray and to turn-of-the-century whites:

[I told them] that the whole future of the Negro rested largely upon the question as to whether or not he should make himself, through his skill, intelligence, and character, of such undeniable value to the community in which he lived that the community could not dispense with his presence. I said that any individual who learned to do something better than anybody else—learned to do a common thing in an uncommon manner—had solved his problem, regardless of the color of his skin.

Now hear Murray, graduate of Tuskegee, in *The Hero and the Blues.* "Heroism, which is, among other things, another word for self-reliance, is not only the indispensible prerequisite for productive citizenship in an open society; it is also that without which no individual or community can remain free."

Both Washington and Du Bois were privately skeptical about the intentions of white people, and both valued heroic leaders. In public they parted company on the efficacy of collective protest. Du Bois's heroes are loudly and collectively resistant; they do not "accept" the fact that they are oppressed. Washington's spend time making sure they improve themselves economically, and in this way help "the black community" by individual achievement. Ultimately Washington is more optimistic about American possibility; he also comes off as a more convinced individualist.

Murray sides with Washington. "I'm not a politican," he says, but like any good citizen, he does have an opinion. He admires the nonviolent strategies associated in this country with Dr. Martin Luther King Jr. "They had a device which would turn the guy's strength against him. I thought that was sophisticated stuff." But he thinks the anticapitalists ruined things. "The rhetoric of Marxism came in. The strategy for recruiting Negroes was a strategy of alienation. Protest and alienation took the way over drive and initiative and go-get-em. See, they wiped out Horatio Alger and the dynamic of the self-made man. Because it was, 'Are you a comrade?' "

Murray told me he would put *Up From Slavery* in the American literary canon because he considers it a representative anecdote. "It's simply Horatio Alger in brown skin! It is the cliché of the times. In other words, I can make it—give me my chance and I will. That's not just the Negro, that's the United States." He pointed to a special brandy he wanted me to try.

Murray's other selections included *The Narrative of the Life of Frederick Douglass* and some of the poetry of Dunbar, though he thinks it's "lightweight." Murray once had an affection for James Weldon Johnson, but now he considers much of his work "light." Certainly, "Ellison would be the most illustrious [Negro] representative." The point is to put forward black individuals who are ready to compete. "We're taking them to Yankee Stadium, man. And you're gonna put Langston Hughes in there with T. S. Eliot? Or Ezra Pound? Or Yeats?"

Murray would select social realist Richard Wright—if Dreiser, Steinbeck, Upton Sinclair had to go in. But "political pamphlets like *The Fire Next Time*," he said, "don't belong in the pantheon." Why *Up From Slavery* and not *The Fire Next Time?* Well . . . never mind the brilliance of Baldwin's technique or the fact that *Up From Slavery* was ghostwritten. "What do you see as representative about *The Fire Next Time?*" he asked.

"I'm not sure that I would use that criterion for putting it into the literary canon." I lifted my glass.

"The biggest impact," he said, "that *The Fire Next Time* had was that it served, alas, to legitimize—to a certain extent for some people—Malcolm X."

I said *Fire* thoroughly criticizes Elijah Muhammed and the Nation. But he didn't hear the objection.

"They don't represent the ancestral imperatives," he says. "The ancestral imperatives are to become American. That's what Frederick Douglass and these guys, to me, represented. One way or the other. One guy takes this route, the other guy takes the other route to do it. One guy says, 'Well, you've got to start down here right with the soil. Then you've got to work your way up and you get your money. If you got enough money, and you got enough power, and you've got enough skill, nobody's going to bother you.' The other guy says, 'No, we've got to have our rights first. We want our dignity and so forth.' The [first] guy says, 'Dignity don't mean shit if you're hungry. You don't have to go around asking him for anything if you've got something he wants.' That's the American way! These guys weren't out there protesting. They were out there going West, getting the Indians out of the way. 'The Indians are in the way, Jack. We *need* this. . . .' I'm not for Sitting Bull winning. I'm for whatever Custer represented. They took it from somebody, somebody took it from them."

Lesson 10: *Albert Murray steps to the plate.*

He wanted to put one in the stands. "Wright was from Mississippi, but he wasn't near Faulkner. Faulkner got some of the most admirable Negroes there ever was. Hardly any Negroes admirable in Richard Wright, you see, and I couldn't find that with Duke, Louis, Count, Jack Johnson, Joe Louis. I got to account for them. Because I was going to be the Joe Louis of literature. Me and Ralph."

Nowhere are Murray's ideas about literature and life more insistently expressed than in his fiction. In *Train Whistle Guitar, The Spyglass Tree,* and *The Seven League Boots* the author offers representative anecdotes which describe the heroic journey of his alter ego, Scooter. Like Murray, Scooter is a native of a small town in Alabama, was a star pupil at Mobile County Training School, attended a college very much like Tuskegee Institute. Scooter is the pride of his hometown and he understands his role at a very early age. He does not betray the trust—Scooter digs the girls, but he also studies hard and succeeds. By the time of the third book in the series, *The Seven League Boots,* Scooter has taken up bass, become an apprentice to a bandleader who is very much like Duke Ellington, then struck out on his own. The books, then, can be seen as part autobiography and part wish fulfillment, and as a flesh-and-blood outline for saving America.

One would hope, however, that Murray's fiction would be more than a mere servant of his theories. Even though his essays never resolve the contradiction between his desire for universality and his stated interest in "saving America," Murray's novels could, like the blues, look beyond either concern to the complexity of actual life. His friend and fellow Tuskegee grad Ralph Ellison's willingness to grow, bend, explore in this way is precisely what made the man such a brilliance. There is a range of opinions in Ellison's work—in *Shadow and Act,* for instance, the writer celebrates the confrontational quality of *Native Son* in "Richard Wright's Blues," and later delivers a careful attack on the shortcomings of the novel, as well as a delineation of his differences from Wright. Ellison, for one, was no polemicist.

Lesson 11: *Albert Murray swings and misses.*

For the most part, his fiction doesn't work. Murray makes Scooter's environment totally subservient to Scooter, to the point of unintentional absurdity—there is no pessimism, no ambiguity, no ambivalence about America the beautiful. Instead, the novelist hands out paean after paean to his own ingenious insights about the ways of Man and the ways black people should act. Here is some wisdom from Scooter in *The Seven League Boots:*

> Most people I know don't know anything at all about the point Booker T. Washington was trying to make when he said what he said in that famous speech. They just take what he said at that point as a very wise old saying about not

overlooking something valuable right under your nose so to speak. To them it goes right along with what old Booker T. also had to say about our people prospering in proportion as we learn to dignify and glorify labor and put brains and skill into the common occupations of life.

That's what it all adds up to for me too, I said, and I also knew a few other things about that historic speech in Atlanta. And I've read the inscription directly from the monument at Tuskegee. But what Booker T.'s bucket always brings to my mind is a church song that goes as far back in my memory as the Sunday school shout that goes "Jesus wants me for a sunbeam."

More trying are Murray's attempts to stitch together the styles of his favorite writers. Faulkner's italicized streams of consciousness, Hemingway's spare attention to detail, Mann's speculative meanderings, Joyce's play with the music of language—it's all in there, absolutely undigested. What's missing most is *novelty*. Murray's desire to talk to the old masters comes at the expense of his characters; Scooter never gets a chance to breathe our air. Instead, he coughs out passages from old classics, which is perfectly reminiscent of the curatorial compositions of too many well-dressed Wyntonites.

Lesson 12: *Albert Murray has the last word.*

There is an irony in the old man's failure to synthesize and improvise and face the truth—the very imprecisions he has railed against in much of his writing. "Craftsmanship does not necessarily add up to artistry," he said during our last talk. "And that's where a lot of people [go wrong]. They look at the notes, they look at the paper, and nobody feels anything for their playing songs, I was playing so and so flat, I did this and the tempo was this. And you say, 'Yeah, OK.' So he's going to try to win a goddamn argument with some intellectual stuff and he's not communicating. Then they want to browbeat you intellectually into it. 'Well, I'm smarter than they are. You can't tell me that because [you don't] know enough about it.' " Whether or not Murray ever notices this failing in himself, his observation makes me a student as much as a critic, and it makes Murray the teacher, perfectly.

When we finished, I gulped down the last of my brandy, the end. Mr. Murray showed some of his old photographs. "That's Jimmy Baldwin." "That's Ralph." "That's Kenneth Burke." I smiled and packed up my recorder. He signed my books and I shouted good-bye to his wife in the bedroom.

He was in the mood for a final lesson. Gesturing toward my hands, the old man said, "These books are serious books. And they keep coming out. None of them is a bestseller [so that] everybody running around [is] talking about Albert Murray. But the sommabitch ain't stopped. He's pretty close to 80. I think that's what you should do. I'm not broke, you know. I'm sharp," he grinned. "I got a pretty wife. Got a million dollars in paintings [by friend Romare Bearden] in sight. All out of serious stuff and no bullshit anywhere."

Downstairs, I opened the pages of the books Stanley Crouch had given me, long ago, when I first started writing for publications. "You should read these," Stanley said back then, handing me his copies of *The Omni-Americans* and *The Hero and the Blues.* I scanned the signatures Albert Murray had left. I particularly liked the one he wrote on the title page of *The Blue Devils of Nada,* gentle reader. "For Joe Wood. Who plays his own riffs on this stuff."

An Intellectual Godfather to Two Generations of Writers, Thinkers, and Artists

Tom Piazza / 1996

From *The Boston Phoenix,* February 23, 1996, section 2, pp. 7–8. Reprinted by permission of Tom Piazza.

Albert Murray's writing desk, which overlooks Manhattan from his Harlem apartment, is dominated by his literary and artistic heroes. Books by Thomas Mann, Ernest Hemingway, James Joyce, and André Malraux compete for space with Robert Graves's *The Greek Myths* and other volumes that explore the connection between storytelling and human consciousness. Behind Murray's desk chair hang large black-and-white photos of Louis Armstrong and Duke Ellington.

In this apartment, he has made at least two generations of artists and writers feel at home—people to whom Murray has served as an intellectual godfather and as something of a hero himself, among them Stanley Crouch, Wynton Marsalis, Cornel West, and Henry Louis Gates Jr.

James Alan McPherson, the Pulitzer Prize-winning author of *Elbow Room,* first met Murray during an early-1970s trip to New York with Michael Harper, Robert Stepto, and Ernest Gaines to interview Ellison. Their quarry turned out to be busy, so Murray showed them around, introducing them to Duke Ellington's sister, Ruth, and bringing them to an exhibit of Romare Bearden's paintings.

"He and Ellison were the two leading black intellectuals in the country at that time," McPherson says. "When they were coming along, they were the trailblazers. Al took me to the Strand Bookstore. He'd say, 'What are you reading on the history of technology?' I'd say, 'Nothing.' He'd say, 'Read this. What are you reading in folklore? Read Joseph Campbell.' Al was there when a lot of us needed instruction, and he gave us what he had."

As essayist, novelist, critic, memoirist, and biographer, Albert Murray has for 30 years lived the role of the black "public intellectual" which has recently been so widely discussed in the media. Yet his work has remained almost unknown to the general public. Perhaps this is because Murray's prose can be knotty and rococo, as challenging to read at times as the densest Faulkner. But more significant, over the past 30 years his vision of this culture has stood outside the main current of African-American writing, placing a heavier emphasis on the second half of that hyphenated term than on the first, and insisting on the notion that African-American life contains more to celebrate than to protest. Too, rather than pushing himself into the forefront of debate, Murray has preferred to read, study, and produce books at his own pace.

Yet that pace is suddenly quickening. This month, Murray has pulled off a formidable literary double-header, the simultaneous publication of a new novel—the third of a trilogy—entitled *The Seven League Boots,* and a major collection of essays on his favorite themes of music and literature, entitled *The Blue Devils of Nada* (both published by Pantheon). In addition, several of his out-of-print books have reappeared, including the memoir *South to a Very Old Place,* which the Modern Library reissued last spring. The public recognition that has eluded him may finally be about to come his way. Or, given the deliberately unfashionable nature of his best work, it may not.

A proud man, Murray seems not to care. From this apartment, where he has lived with his wife, Mozelle, and daughter, Michele, for the past 33 years, Murray regards the rest of Manhattan, and the world, with a combination of persistent, pragmatic optimism, which he seems to feel almost obliged to uphold, and a subtler, less apparent pessimism that he keeps camouflaged. The two qualities often appear to be at war, and they lend his work much of its characteristic tension.

Murray's two-bedroom apartment is bright and comfortable; he receives guests warmly, although he is hampered now by a debilitating back problem that has all but confined him to a wheelchair. He is slight and wiry, with a pencil-thin mustache; in conversation he is animated, forceful, and sometimes irascible, with the level of engagement of a much younger man. He gives the impression that he is anxious not to be misunderstood, and his expression slides easily from delight into annoyance, from peevishness into conspiratorial irony.

Murray betrays particular impatience at any apparent attempt to define him by his ethnic background.

"The arts," he says, "help you to see yourself in the broadest context of what it means to be a human being. Idiomatic variations—whether someone is Italian, or Irish, or African, or 'African-American'—are not fundamental.

A writer tries to take the idiomatic and, through form, make it a part of the heritage of humanity at large."

The tension, and cooperation, between that "broad context" and the specific idioms of black America has been at the heart of Murray's work from the beginning. It was literature that provided Murray with much of his early aspiration to escape from Magazine Point, Alabama, a small town on the outskirts of Mobile where he was born in 1916. That became the fictional setting of Gasoline Point in Murray's first novel, *Train Whistle Guitar* (McGraw-Hill, 1974). Despite the lyrical rendering of the South in several of his books, Murray seems to have had a deep sense of being in a backwater. "Entropy," he says, "was the nothingness of Gasoline Point."

The desire to escape such "entropy" propelled him to the Tuskegee Institute in 1935, where Murray was exposed to a widening world of arts and literature, and became acquainted with an upperclassman named Ralph Ellison. They met again when Murray came to do graduate work at New York University after a stint in the Air Force during World War II. From that point on, the two had a strong mutual influence, which pointed toward a vision of American society rooted in folklore, American literature, the improvisatory nature of jazz, and the ritual-based, celebratory aspects of black life. "We became very, very close friends," Murray says. "He was working on *Invisible Man* and reading it to me. I was the person, it turned out, with whom he could operate on the most levels. Some of the New York people said that Ralph became more and more Southern once I got to New York."

In New York, and during a long summer in Paris in 1950, Murray established friendships with artists, writers, and intellectuals like Clement Greenberg, James Baldwin, Anaïs Nin, Romare Bearden, Maya Deren, Joseph Campbell, and Francis Steegmuller. Yet while his schoolmate Ellison was writing *Invisible Man* and the essays in *Shadow and Act,* Murray spent most of the 1950s back in the Air Force, from which he retired in 1962 with the rank of major, publishing only occasionally. It wasn't until he moved to Harlem in 1962 that his writing career began to pick up momentum, as he published a series of essays for *Life, Harper's,* and other magazines. These were eventually collected in his first book, *The Omni-Americans,* which was published in 1970. Murray was 54.

The Omni-Americans, when it appeared, stood apart from the stream of militant books by African-American authors that had appeared in the 1960s, such as Eldridge Cleaver's *Soul on Ice* and Claude Brown's *Manchild in the Promised Land,* both of which Murray criticized in *The Omni-Americans.*

What set his work apart was Murray's insistence that American culture is "mulatto"—not a mosaic, and certainly not a homogeneous white culture containing equally homogeneous black "ghettos."

The Omni-Americans included witty and original critiques of Gunnar Myrdal's *An American Dilemma,* the Moynihan Report, the writings of James Baldwin, and other manifestations of what Murray called a "folklore of black pathology." Rather than pathology, he argued, the black American experience evinces nothing so much as an amazing resilience and elegance that he classed with mankind's great heroic and aesthetic achievements. Against the protest tradition he posed the blues tradition, which he characterized not as lamentation but as a music of elegant confrontation.

"Murray's work," Cornel West says, "shows the radically hybrid character of American civilization. He provides a way of exploding all these simplistic pluralism models, and of reaching a deeper historical understanding of the ways in which American culture as a whole has been shaped by African-Americans."

Perhaps not surprisingly, *The Omni-Americans* wasn't to the taste of a public that increasingly wanted its racial politics painted in primary colors and dotted with exclamation points. Two years after the book's publication, Walker Percy, musing in the *Tulane Law Review* on why it wasn't better known, observed that it fell "into a kind of ideological no-man's land."

"Show me a book," Percy wrote, "about race and the United States that fits no ideology, resists all abstractions, offends orthodox liberals and conservatives, attacks social scientists and Governor Wallace in the same breath, sees all the failures of the country and holds out hope in the end—then I have to sit up and take notice." He concluded by claiming that *The Omni-Americans* "may well be the most important book on white-black relations in the United States, indeed on American culture, published in this generation."

Although the general reading public was asleep to it, Murray's work did not go completely unnoticed; it was during this period that younger black writers such as Crouch, McPherson, and John Edgar Wideman came to see Murray's sensibility as a kind of benchmark, and began to congregate at his apartment.

Over the next few years, Murray produced a series of books that gained him a powerful underground reputation, including the widely admired *South to a Very Old Place,* a memoir and travelogue which deals with changes in the Deep South; *Train Whistle Guitar,* which uses folkloric elements in a loosely woven growing-up story; and the extremely influential *Stomping the*

Blues, an extended meditation on the metaphysics of jazz music, which casts blues-idiom music and the "Saturday Night Functions" where it was played as a kind of community purification ritual.

Certain critical, philosophical, and ideological riffs recur throughout Murray's books. They include a disposition toward "heroic action" as opposed to protest or lamentation; a belief that art—and especially literature—doesn't just express values but creates them; and an insistence that African-American (a term he doesn't like, preferring "Negro American") experience is at the heart of American experience. Around these themes Murray spins a rich netting of allusion and cross-reference, set into a densely textured prose that argues for a view of life in the United States impossible to categorize as "conservative," "Afrocentric," or any other catch phrase.

"Al believes that the point of literature is both to entertain and to instruct," says Wideman. "He believes that the tie between art and culture is real and important, and that what is thought and written in a culture is serious business. On a superficial level, part of his point of view might almost seem conservative, but if you look at the values that inform his work, they are on the side of imagination, possibility, innovation, and transformation."

Indeed, in a culture in which blame-throwing has become a national pastime, Murray's focus on self-determination as opposed to the redress of grievances may be seen as conservative. But, as he says, "I don't see how my main purpose in being put on this earth could be to protest white people, man."

In a real sense, Murray's life values are his aesthetic values, and his aesthetic values are ethical values as well. "Art," he says, "is a movement against entropy. Its ends are sanity, purpose, and delight. It stems from ritual; it gives ideals and goals. When you lose that—when you get a nihilistic view of life—then you're in trouble. Without the discipline that ultimately comes from the arts, civilization could blow up any day.

"The whole basis of my writing," he says, "lies in the literary implications of the blues. The blues is another word for entropy. In playing the blues, a musician heroically confronts entropy with grace and style. The more 'don't care-ified' you are, the more effectively you dispel the blues. Adversity is a constant in life, and the dragon is always bigger than the hero.

"Racism is not going to disappear," he goes on. "So you can't measure things in terms of high-school idealism. You've got to show me something worse than a few skinheads jumping out there saying 'we're gonna blow them away.' Because I'll show you Gore and Clinton. As far as I can see, those are the most shining products of the civil-rights movement. Those guys don't have any distance between themselves and Negroes of achievement. They're used to being around them, they put them in responsible positions.

"You've got to look at real change," he says. "Even if you're the head of the skinheads, if your son wants a pair of basketball sneakers, you better get him some Air Jordans."

Yet underneath Murray's constant affirmation of morale lurks a pained awareness of the ways in which, in his view, the social contract has been eroded in the United States. "Societies, like individuals, need to have something in focus that is an integral human value. If the only value is freedom of self-indulgence, it doesn't take much to see you're headed for chaos. Obviously there is a decline in civility and morality across the board. With that comes all the elements that lead to xenophobia and ethnocentrism. It's not just in racial matters. All that nobility that we developed in the 1960s went the way of the other nobilities."

Murray's own extended literary project, a trilogy about a young man named Scooter, begun in *Train Whistle Guitar,* continued in *The Spyglass Tree,* and culminating in this month's *The Seven League Boots,* is his way of addressing the need he sees for heroic images in fiction. He refers to his fiction as "fairy tales set to Ellington orchestration," the goals of which are to "create an idealized American type, an image that is rich enough for readers to aspire to."

In light of Murray's own belief that tragedy has an important role in creating heroes in fiction, his novels suffer, perhaps, from an overly strong impulse to stimulate morale in readers. Scooter is a talented lad whose intelligence and high-mindedness are never in doubt, to himself or to anybody else. He never questions, and, more important, the novel's terms never question, the ultimate values of achievement, optimism, and self-reliance.

The dragons, whether internal or external, that usually inhabit fairy tales are offstage in these books, and Scooter never has to deal with the kinds of painful realizations that, say, the protagonist of *Invisible Man,* or even your basic blues singer, must confront. When asked about this, Murray shrugs. "I don't deal with that aspect of life. You don't criticize a dentist for not being an internist. If you're John Philip Sousa, you're not Beethoven."

Whether a large public will decide to march to Murray's fictional beat or not, his largest achievement almost certainly lies in his original and brilliant essays. The title of his new essay collection, *The Blue Devils of Nada,* nods in the direction both of the blues, which have inspired so much of Murray's work, and Ernest Hemingway's story "A Clean, Well-Lighted Place." The book is a worthy successor to *The Omni-Americans* and the extended essays in *The Hero and the Blues* and *Stomping the Blues*. In it, Murray evolves a highly personal aesthetic program that uses as its touchstones the work of Hemingway and Duke Ellington. It is a fascinating and important collection that brings together all of Murray's central themes and preoccupations.

Although Murray's extraordinary Indian summer obviously pleases him, he regards it with no outsize hopes for his books' effect either on his own life or on the society he cares about so passionately. "Ultimately," he says, "I believe in 'vanity of vanities, all is vanity.' I don't think that anything means anything, unless you make it mean something. You know, all civilizations end up getting *dug* up . . . "

As he says this, the light of conspiratorial irony enters his eye again. Perhaps referring to our culture, perhaps to his own mortality, he adds, "We can't know how many choruses we have left to play. Maybe it's 50, maybe it's 15. But even if we only have five, let's make them swing. Right?"

Murray, a Great Black Hope at 79, Stomps on Literary Establishment

Michael J. Agovino / 1996

From *The New York Observer,* March 4, 1996, pp. 1, 19. Reprinted by permission of Michael J. Agovino.

Albert Murray is talking—vamping, really—about days gone by.

"So, I was in Paris, this was years ago, in 1950," he said in a lilting Southern rasp, sitting uptown in his eighth-floor apartment on 132nd Street. "And I was joking with a hotel concierge in French and some guy says, 'Damn, you from down in Alabama and you're a colored boy and you're up here making jokes.' And I'm this and I'm that. He wasn't arrogant, just incredulous. So I said, 'What makes you think you're smarter than me? I'm a smart boy!' "

He let out a big, warm, avuncular laugh. "People like that are just *not knowing,*" he said.

"Not knowing" is the kind of bluesy, out-of-kilter word coupling that, if he were better known, might be described as *Murrayesque.* And with seven books to his name and his third novel, *The Seven League Boots,* and a book of essays, *The Blue Devils of Nada,* just out from Pantheon, this could turn out to be the year of Albert Murray's renaissance.

"Somebody like him," said writer and Murray disciple Stanley Crouch in an excited falsetto, "deserves at least as much attention as Norman Mailer gets when his books come out."

Despite consistently good reviews over his 26-year writing career, Mr. Murray, who turns 80 on Mother's Day, has never been able to crack the literary opinion-makers. The literati have only so many slots allotted for black writers, and those who are the keepers of the canon haven't found the time to give Mr. Murray a seat at their table.

Take, for instance, Harold Bloom, guardian of the Western canon, inhaler of 1,000 pages an hour.

"Ah, yes, I knew Albert at the Century Club," he said, wearily. "He was a very charming and delightful man, but I haven't read any fiction by him. Are there one or two novels? I did read that very fine history of jazz, a very

117

moving and elegant book, and I've read another book by Albert, but what was it, dear?"

Alfred Kazin remembered eating dinner at the Murrays' once, he said, but as for his writing, he had no opinion. "Which work are we talking about?" he asked. "Offhand, I can't recall Albert Murray's work."

"As I wrote in *The Blue Devils of Nada,*" Mr. Murray said, "most of these guys think if you're not pissing and moaning about civil rights that you don't have anything to say and that, basically, I'm invading their territory. Way down underneath they resent it. They want you to be a colored boy out there bitching. That's why they miss the ambiguity in *Invisible Man.* They'll always say, 'This guy's complaining that nobody sees him.' It's deeper than that; but they can always get away with it on that level because it looks like victimization again and, in the end [of the novel] he says, 'I might also be talkin' about you.' " He laughed again. "It could be *you,* Jack."

Albert Murray's apartment is teeming with hundreds of CDs, thousands of records—Blind Lemon Jefferson, Antonin Dvorak, Louis Armstrong, Franz Joseph Haydn, Ray Charles, even an Ernest Hemingway reading—and books. First editions of T. S. Eliot, William Faulkner and Thomas Mann share space alongside Jo Jones' drumsticks, and all of it sits in a room with a view of midtown that network sitcoms would be jealous of, if it weren't in Harlem. Then there are the Romare Bearden paintings—a watercolor in the living room, a sketch in the study, a lithograph in the foyer, a collage in the bathroom—15 originals in all.

"It can be looked upon as an embodiment of the information superhighway," Mr. Murray said. "All this space has to do with how much I can learn about the world."

For an adopted child, born in 1916 down in "the Beel" (Mobile, Ala.), Albert Lee Murray has learned a lot about the world. From "the Beel," he went to the Tuskegee Institute in the late 30s, where he struck up a friendship with Ralph Ellison. After that came the Air Force, from which he retired as a major in 1962 to study and teach his way through a number of universities across the country. And then he began writing.

Mr. Murray has produced a formidable body of work. His first book, the polemical culture dissection *The Omni-Americans,* marked him in 1970 as an individual thinker, rather than a mouthpiece for white bleeding hearts or Afrocentrists. Over the next 25 years, it was followed by a succession of important and distinctly American literary works: the slim but weighty *The Hero and the Blues,* an extended essay in which he equated the Western literary protagonist to the blues musician; his first novel, *Train Whistle Guitar,* about the coming of age of his semiautobiographical hero, Scooter; "that very fine history of jazz," as Mr. Bloom put it, *Stomping the Blues,* a seminal redefinition of the blues idiom; a collaboration with William (Count) Basie on the bandleader's autobiography; and his second novel, *The Spyglass Tree,* which even Michiko Kakutani liked.

His leitmotif is always *the blues*—the blues not being pangs of victimization, but something more metaphysical, something to be conquered with style and improvisation and, thus, life-affirming. It's a profound idea in a time when profundities are hard to come by.

Still, the author has been dogged by the fact that each of his books has managed to go out of print at one time or another. "It has to bother you on one level," he said, "because you're involved in trying to communicate. Like Duke once said, 'If people don't listen, we're in trouble. We're playing music and we want it to be heard.' "

Mr. Crouch attributes the problem in part to the long layoff between *Stomping the Blues* in 1976 and the Basie autobiography in 1985, but he also scolds "the so-called black studies departments on campuses that turn out to be ideologically driven and commanded by second-rate thinkers, most of whom are incapable of addressing what Murray is laying down."

But well-meaning white liberals haven't addressed "what Murray is laying down," either. In fact, in *The Omni-Americans,* Mr. Murray dismissed such do-gooders, and in his 1972 memoir and Modern Library Book, *South to a Very Old Place,* he put it this way: "Self-styled color-blind white Americans who obviously assume that they must pretend to ignore differences in order to avoid conflict only add hypocrisy to already existing complications."

"I've talked to many different people about Albert Murray and why he doesn't get the recognition, so this is like a broken record," said novelist John Edgar Wideman, sounding a bit impatient. "It's a mystery inside an enigma. African-American art is something a lot of folks go to for a kind of break—for fun—which is fine, but Albert Murray emphasizes the work behind the fun. . . . We can have an Albert Murray boom tomorrow, but it wouldn't mean his writing is any better or accessible or more significant. It would just mean the kind of lottery or bingo game of media attention has settled on him and he'll have his week and disappear."

As an intellectual, Mr. Murray considers himself part of no camp. "I'm telling you how to be an American," he said. "I'm out there saying, 'I can make a better American out of you than *he* can.' "

Just when you think he's a trumpet for neoconservatism, he'll tell you that O. J. Simpson was *not* guilty or that he enjoyed *Waiting to Exhale.* But then he'll refer to Afrocentrism as "off-the-wall bullshit." And don't get him started on rap music.

"It's square to me," he said, "the beat is square, the words are square. I mean, it's amazing. You expect progress, but this is not progress. These guys sound like they're two years away from slavery. Like 'Knockin' the Bones'— you know that song?" For a second, he becomes a human beat box. "*A ba ba ba. A bee boom ba.* There's nothing swinging about *that.* It's just not hip."

For all his talk of the past—of friends like "Duke," "Count," "Romey," "Ralph"—he's not a sentimentalist. "Oh, yeah, I miss 'em; you know how that goes," he mumbled, keeping a stiff upper lip before breaking into dead-on impressions of Ellington and Armstrong. Only when he plays Jelly Roll Morton's "Kansas City Stomp"—he often plays a tune or reads a bit of Hemingway to illustrate a point—do his eyes well up.

"There," he said, pointing into space, "I can see the infield, the pennants blowing in the wind. I can smell the Spaulding glove."

A siren blared on Lenox Avenue, and he came back. "That's my Proustian madeleine," he said.

Mr. Murray is, above all, gentlemanly—to a fault, sometimes. He serves as a kind of éminence grise to Mr. Crouch and Wynton Marsalis, who head up the Jazz at Lincoln Center program, and last December, he took part in a panel discussion on early jazz pioneer James Europe. At times, the lecture was downright stultifying, desperate for someone to bring it to life. But Dan Morgenstern, the director of the Institute of Jazz Studies at Rutgers University, barely let Mr. Murray, or anyone else for that matter, have their say. And that was that. After the lecture, it was Albert Murray everyone gathered round.

Back in his apartment, besides his books and records, there are his photo albums. Mr. Murray in a Venice gondola, 1950; Major Murray in Morocco; with Arthur Miller at Rose and William Styron's house; with Sugar Ray Robinson, shagging flies on a baseball diamond; with James Baldwin in Antibes, standing there, like Jack Kerouac in the Gap ads, wearing khakis. Of course, it is Mr. Murray who accomplished what the Beats set out to do: meld the rhythms of jazz with words. It's one of his great achievements, though he's never been given credit for it.

Sitting in his living room, wearing his clunky, black-framed glasses, his right index finger pointing up to the sky, he rang out:

> There was a chinaberry tree in the front yard of that house in those days, and in early spring the showers outside that window always used to become pale green again. Then before long there would be chinaberry blossoms. Then it would be maytime and then junebugtime and no more school bell mornings until next September. . . .

"You can hear those words swing," said Duke Ellington's nephew, Michael James. "His sentences are in four-four time." Or in three-four or six-eight; he's got phrasings and syncopations as irregular as a Satchel Paige windup.

"He creates rhythms that jump right out at you," said downtown tenor saxophonist David Murray, who composed an ebullient, ever so dissonant 12-minute piece for his octet after reading *Train Whistle Guitar*. "I heard his voice when I read that book, and it's music, man, it's definitely music."

But Mr. Murray is writing music about a world that doesn't exist anymore. He keeps on, though, the epitome of grace under pressure, looking for affirmation in the face of adversity.

"The question," Mr. Murray said, vamping again, "is whether life is worth living. Are you going to wake up one morning and cut your throat or go stomping at the Savoy?" He answers in a rousing vibrato. *"You know what I'm goin' do!"*

The Omni-American

Tony Scherman / 1996

From *American Heritage* 47, no. 5 (September 1996), pp. 68–77. Reprinted by permission of *American Heritage*.

At Albert Murray's request, material that was originally a part of his interview with Mr. Scherman but which did not appear in the version published in *American Heritage* has been included in brackets. The reinstated material primarily represents additions to the text. Occasionally, a substitution is included. In the latter case, both that which was originally published and the substitution are offered.

Albert Murray sees American culture as an incandescent fusion of European, Yankee, frontier, and black. And he sees what he calls the "blues idiom" as the highest expression of that culture.

When he was seventy, Albert Murray scuttled around Manhattan with the energy of a far younger man. A decade later, two spinal operations having cruelly diminished his orbit, Murray needs one of those four-pronged aluminum canes to inch down a sidewalk, bitter punishment for a naturally impatient man. Albert Murray's big, handsome grin, which turns a listener into a coconspirator in whatever iconoclasm he is hatching at the moment, gets flashed less often now. Still, Murray keeps his pique pretty much under control (there is too much to do). One day last summer he journeyed to a lower Fifth Avenue show room. Since Murray spends most of his time in chairs, a good one is vitally important. "Something," he said, disarming the suave salesman with that smile, "something that'll let me write two, three more books."

Albert Murray didn't publish a book until he was fifty-four. A fellow who prides himself on being at home anywhere in the Western world, a connoisseur of Paris's sights and sounds as well as New York's, he was too busy accumulating experiences and perceptions to work at getting them down on paper. When he finally did, the books came in a flood, nine in twenty-five years: the essay collection *The Omni-Americans* (1970); the autobiographical travelogue *South to a Very Old Place* (1971); three lectures on art titled *The Hero and the Blues* (1973); an essay on jazz called *Stomping the Blues*

122

(1976); *Good Morning Blues,* Count Basie's autobiography, as told to Murray (1985); a fictional trilogy, *Train Whistle Guitar* (1974), *The Spyglass Tree* (1991), and *The Seven League Boots* (just published); and a second essay collection, *The Blue Devils of Nada,* also just out.

In a fairer world (which he doesn't expect; life, he loves to repeat, is nothing but a "low-down dirty shame"), Albert Lee Murray, who became an octogenarian last May, would be prized as one of our great men of letters, a polymath whose immediate concerns may be American culture and jazz music, but whose glance takes in the entire sweep of Western history, literature, and art. To the extent that Murray is known, it is as the theorist of (and coiner of the term) *omni-Americanism,* which holds that American culture is composite at its core, that black and white Americans are each other's cultural ancestors. But Murray's ideas about our common heritage, as fascinating and fruitful as they are, are a mere byproduct of his primary goal: to understand the nature of art and to defend artistic activity as a basic, utterly indispensable response to the human condition.

Murray's life story doesn't strike him as improbable, though it is; to him it's just a piece of what he calls "America's incontestably mulatto culture." Born out of wedlock in 1916, he was adopted by an Alabama working couple and given a happy childhood in a neighborhood outside Mobile known as Magazine Point. Bright and curious, he was earmarked early by teachers and sent to the Mobile County Training School (whose principal, Benjamin Francis Baker, was the sort of model of passionate turn-of-the-century rectitude Murray's life-long friend Ralph Ellison repeatedly memorialized in essays: ramrod-straight educators, the sons and daughters of slaves, tirelessly and in near-total obscurity steering the grandchildren of slaves into America's mainstream).

Booker T. Washington was only two decades dead when Murray enrolled in Washington's school, the Tuskegee Institute (Ellison, a mysterious, alluring upperclassman, was already there), where he would later teach. Losing himself in the library stacks, he devoured the entire Western canon—but especially Mann, Joyce, Proust, Hemingway, Malraux, and Faulkner, cultivating, meanwhile, an expert taste in what was then black popular music— Ellington's, Basie's, and Armstrong's jazz—and becoming as much of a fashion plate as limited means allowed. He saw no incongruity in a black crosstie-cutter's son from Alabama aspiring to the literate elegance he pored over in the pages of his favorite magazine, the then brand-new *Esquire.*

Murray used a career in the Air Force (he left a major) to become a world traveler. Stationed in Morocco in the mid-fifties, he hopped the Mediterranean to Paris, Rome, and Athens, sampling their cafés and cultural treasures. Shipped to Massachusetts, he became a habitué of Cambridge jazz- and book-loving circles. He already had haunted late-forties Manhattan while earning a master's degree at New York University.

In 1962 he and his wife, Mozelle, and daughter, Michele, settled in New York City. There he remained, pursuing his writer's vocation in earnest and cultivating friendships with New York-based jazz musicians from Ellington to Wynton Marsalis, whose intellectual development Murray has overseen in almost fifteen years of discussions, arguments, and bull sessions. Murray serves on the board of directors of Jazz at Lincoln Center, which doesn't begin to indicate his impact on the influential concert series. He is its philosopher-in-residence.

Murray's thought isn't hard to summarize; one of the admirable things about the set of ideas he unshyly calls Cosmos Murray is that it *is* a cosmos. His views add up to a cohesive, elegant whole, making him a rarity in today's attenuated intellectual world: a system builder, a visionary in the grand manner.

He grounds his thought in the notion of literature as "equipment for living," not a disinterested contemplation of the world but an active engagement with it. The basic literary motive, says Murray—storytelling—inheres in every human being; indeed, without inventing stories and metaphors to order our raw experience, we would be unable to function. The artist, playing, improvising, shaping, becomes the model for the rest of us, who struggle to wrest meaning from the flux and chaos that underpin our lives, our brief term on earth. The artists with the clearest vision of the nothingness at the heart of human existence, Hemingway, Mann, and Malraux, make up Murray's pantheon, into which he inducts a fourth member, Ellington.

Jazz, in fact, provides Murray with his key concept, the "blues idiom," a phrase he uses to describe both his heroes' artistic method and their unsentimental view of the world. For him, blues idiom has a double meaning. On the one hand, it connects with "down-home Negro USA," the Deep Southern birthplace of the blues and jazz, but on the other, it transcends ethnic connotations. It is the aesthetic of the novelist, painter, or jazz musician who has mastered the high-wire act of affirming his existence, of celebrating himself, in the face of adversity. Adversity might be the grinding misery of Negro slavery or the lack of meaning modern, existential man sees at the root of all life. Life may be pointless, but it is nonetheless livable if approached with the courage and physical grace of a Hemingway toreador, or the novelist's shaping eye, or the jazz musician's joy in pulling beauty, wit, and meaning from thin air. For Murray, any great artist is doing the same thing; keeping what he calls the blue devils of *nada* at bay.

That is the central idea of the small book that underlies Murray's entire project, *The Hero and the Blues,* whose final chapter, "The Blues and the Fable in the Flesh," is as exciting a piece of intellectual trailblazing as anything written in the last quarter-century. Murray's coupling of jazz with literature—with all the fine arts, via their defining activity, the improvising creativity of the human mind—is a lasting achievement and one that likely will be built on by others in years to come.

In the end Murray may endure more as a thinker than as a novelist (he would strenuously disagree; he sees himself as a writer of fiction). In any case, his best prose is wonderful indeed. Jazz isn't just a source of ideas for Murray; he has worked hard to model the rhythms of his sentences on those of jazz. His best-written books, *Train Whistle Guitar* and *South to a Very Old Place,* are studded with the rolling cadences of down-home speech, perfectly grasped.

In *South to a Very Old Place* he imitates the child-loving, baby-talking women he grew up surrounded by, sliding, sentence by sentence, into high-grade nonsense: "Play the little man for Mama, Albert Lee. Just play the little man for Mama. That's all right about that old booger man. You just be the little man for Mama. You just be my little Mister Buster Brown man. Mama's little Buster Brown man ain't scared of no booger man and nothing else. Mama's little man ain't scared of nobody and nothing in creation, or tarnation either. Because Mama's little man is Mama's BIG man, just like him daddy that's what him is. That's exactly what him is, betchem bones. Him momom Mittchem Buttchem Bwown. Momoms itchem bittchem Mittchem Buttchem Bwown; betchem tweet bones."

In nine books, irrespective of genre—in *South to a Very Old Place,* with its stylish, playful flow, in *Train Whistle Guitar,* with its knottily graceful, razor-sharp evocations, in *Stomping the Blues,* driving home its argument in one subtly shaded verbal riff after another, in *The Hero and the Blues* and its merciless logic, in these and his other works—Murray has made his mark for the ages.

TS: Let's start with some of your basic ideas. Tell me about your concept of the different levels of artistic activity.

AM: Sure. Art is the process by which raw experience is stylized into aesthetic statement. Now, that process can take place on three levels. There's the folk level, which is the illiterate level. There's the pop level, which has the widest appeal. It can range from the folk to the most highly refined, so the pop artist has the broadest resources, but his bane is ephemerality. The highest level is fine art. That's the ultimate extension, elaboration, and refinement. If you understand what goes into creating jazz, the degree of sophistication involved, you realize that it's a fine art.

TS: But jazz has its origins in the first, folk level.

AM: Of course. Everything starts there. Bach and Beethoven, Shakespeare and Goethe came out of barbarians and peasants, those Celts and Saxons and people from the steppes. It *all* starts on an ignorant level. As you develop a greater mastery of your means of stylization—more technique, more sophistication in your perceptions—you move to another level. When jazz was *the* popular music, Duke Ellington was writing "Echoes of Harlem," which goes beyond popular music. Somewhat like Shakespeare, who was writing popular plays—otherwise he couldn't have gotten that many people into the theater—but whose development took him beyond pop feedback into the realm of sophisticated taste and intellectual refinement.

TS: You see the artist as an educator.

AM: Yes. Here's a quotation from my book *The Hero and the Blues*: "As he turns page after page, following the fortunes of the storybook hero, the reader is as deeply engaged in the educative process as if he were an apprentice in a workshop. Indeed, he is an apprentice, and his workshop includes the whole range of human possibility and endeavor. His task is to learn from the example of journeymen and master craftsmen such skills as not only will enable him to avoid confusion and destruction, but also will enhance his own existence as well as that of human beings everywhere."

TS: What is your quarrel with the social sciences as the basis of education?

AM: Oversimplification of motive. Questionable underlying assumptions. The social function of literature, of all art, is to help the individual come to terms with himself upon the earth, to help him confront the deepest, most complex questions of life. You see? The human proposition! If you deal with sociological concepts, you never deal with the basic complexity of life. You reduce everything to social and political problems, stuff like whether or not the red ants like the brown ants. The storyteller is not someone who tries to solve a voting problem or some type of social problem. The guy wasn't trying to solve some political problem in Elizabethan England when he was writing *Hamlet.* You get what I'm saying?

When you look at the deeper and much more complicated personal problems, you'll find that the oldest answers are still the answers. There's nothing outdated about fairy tales, about legends, about the religious holy books, and so forth. When you know how to decode them and apply them to your life— well, you approach wisdom.

TS: What's an example of a novel that you would fault as having a social science point of view? Richard Wright's *Native Son?*

AM: Exactly. It's based on Marxist ideology. It's based on the idea that an oppressed person will become a dangerous animal. Where does Murray take issue with that? Murray's got what he thinks is a more basic concept— that you also can be *made,* or developed, not simply destroyed, by adversity. In other words, the concept of antagonistic cooperation. No dragons, no heroes; no temptations, no saints.

TS: What is the blues idiom?

AM: It's an attitude of affirmation in the face of difficulty, of improvisation in the face of challenge. It means you acknowledge that life is a low-down dirty shame yet confront that fact with perseverance, with humor, and, above all, with elegance.

I've called the blues idiom "part of the existential equipment that we Americans inherited from our captive ancestors." Who has suffered the greatest foul play of the people who came to America? The Negro, right? There's a richness in the Negro response to adversity. There is resilience, inventiveness, humor, and enviable elegance. We invented the blues; Europeans invented psychoanalysis ["Europeans invented" replaced with the following: good time music, not psychoanalysis]. You invent what you need. And when I say "our captive ancestors," I'm talking to all Americans. The blues is white Americans' heritage too. That's why they can identify with something that is so idiomatically down-home brownskin as jazz.

TS: Does blues music reflect the feeling called the blues?

AM: The blues as such is depression, melancholia, despair, disintegration, sadness. Blues as music is a way of making an aesthetic statement with

sound. It swings! Its insouciance and elegance are the best antidote for the
blues as such. The conventional American thinks blues music is sad. That's
hillbilly music; hillbilly music is crying music. Conventional Americans
think Negroes are crying when they're singing the blues. They're not; they're
getting ready to have a good time!

TS: What does your term *omni-Americans* mean?

AM: It reflects my basic assumption that the United States is a mulatto
culture. First, let's put things in a world context. Go back to what [the French
poet] Paul Valéry called *Homo europaeus,* a composite of Greek logic,
Roman administration, and Judeo-Christian morality. That's what makes a
European different from somebody in India, Japan, or Africa. Now send him
across the Atlantic. You get what [the American author] Constance Rourke
identified in *American Humor*—a book, by the way, that has the status of a
bible with me—as a new composite: of the ingenious Yankee, the frontiersman, who's part Indian, and the Negro. *All* Americans, I don't care if it's a
neo-Nazi, are part Yankee, part backwoodsman, part Negro.

So that's the definition of American culture: *Homo europaeus* with an
overlay of this new composite. American culture is the cutting edge of European culture, and the most effective, most sophisticated stylization of the
American spirit is found in jazz.

TS: So we are all omni-Americans?

AM: All of us. The omni-Americans are the Americans. My conception
makes Americans identify with *all* their ancestors. It lets me ["lets me" replaced with the following: enables me to] identify with John Jay, you with
Frederick Douglass.

Incidentally, once you start looking for examples of mulatto culture, you
find some fascinating ones. Will Marion Cook, for instance, was a student of
Dvořák in the 1890s, who put Dvořák in touch with Negro spirituals and later
became one of Duke Ellington's mentors. That's a perfect example of omni-
Americanism. You can trace a line from Dvořák, the epitome of the classical
European composer, through Will Marion Cook to Duke Ellington.

TS: Doesn't this bring us to the late John Kouwenhoven, whose *The Beer
Can by the Highway* and *Made in America* are two more of your bibles?

AM: Yes, it does. Kouwenhoven's concept is that American culture comes
from the interaction of vernacular or folk tradition with learned or academic
tradition. For instance, Ellington realized that to create an arrangement that
showcased a soloist like, say, Armstrong, was to make an American concerto.

TS: I'd never thought of it in those terms—the jazz solo as the American concerto.

AM: Of course! What is a concerto? A showcase for a solo instrument. And isn't the cocktail lounge, the after-hours joint, the gin mill the obvious source of American chamber music?

Anyway, what few if any of Kouwenhoven's readers seem to have understood is that this interaction occurs within the context of free enterprise. Don't reduce it to economics; I'm talking about free endeavor: an experimental attitude, an openness to improvisation. The disposition to approach life as a frontiersman, you see, so piety does not hold you back. You can't be over-respectful of established forms; you're trying to get through the wilderness to Kentucky. I'm not talking about a royal road to Rome; I'm going to Kentucky, and I've got all these goddamned redskins to mess with! Do you see what I mean? It's open-minded experimentation, and you don't have it anywhere else; you only have it in America. The interaction of French, Italian, German, and English music with African music by itself doesn't add up to jazz. The synthesis needs our context of free enterprise.

Underlying everything else in jazz is the concept "All men are created equal." The blues is not the creation of a crushed-spirited people; it's the product of a forward-looking, upward-striving people. Jazz is only possible in a climate of freedom.

TS: Wait a minute. Slavery? Racism? That's a climate of freedom?

AM: Nowhere in the world that I know about but America is everybody born saying, "Anybody up there in the government is there through the consent of the governed. We can kick the rascals out at any time." O.K., you had a side issue: "Well, these people have a different color skin." But Negroes were not less American than anybody else. They expected the same thing [: equal access to educational and political institutions, freedom from official segregation].

TS: But there was—is—a huge contradiction between the ideology of equality and the reality.

AM: That's not as important as you might think. We got all those Negroes segregated? That's unimportant, compared with the fact that they shouldn't be. It's not the fact that they're segregated but the fact that if they were segregated in another society, it wouldn't even matter. Can't you see that?

What was guaranteed to the average dirt farmer in England by the Magna Carta? Who cared about peasants in Russia, including after communism made them more peasant than ever? What did the French small farmer get from the Revolution? He didn't grow up with the heritage every American has.

TS: In other words, the Constitution was, and is, an explosive ideology. It promises freedom.

AM: Right. The point is: The promises, the guarantees of the Constitution became the birthright of all Americans. That's what is important. If you had a million slaves, it didn't mean the same thing as if you didn't have these guarantees. [Previous sentence deleted.] Were they free in Africa? They were owned by their chief. The first they ever heard of freedom as a right was over here. Blacks ["Blacks" replaced with the following: Those people] weren't complaining for all those years about being taken away from Africa; they were complaining about being excluded from full participation in American society. Also, what the "Back-to-Africa" spokesmen visualized was an American social system, not a traditional African one. The important thing is that the official promise existed: "All men are created equal." Now you had something to appeal to.

TS: How do you see yourself first, as American or as black?

AM: I can't separate those things. I'm an American, that's all. I was already an American before I was ever conscious that I was black. I was already breathing, I was already hearing railroad trains, I was already hearing sawmill whistles, I was already hearing automobiles, I was hearing the English language. I looked around and saw all these different people, and they looked like people that belonged around me. Some of them were white, some of them were Indian, some of them were Creole, and so on. That some talked one way and some another seemed natural. That there were conflicts also seemed natural. Conflicts exist just about everywhere.

When I hear the term *black writer,* certain alarms go off. Remember, the last thing I want to be mistaken for is a spokesman. If I'm not one of the best living American writers, no thanks for being one of the best living black writers. I'm trying to make sense of all American culture, using the Hemingway principle of writing about what you know about. You achieve universality through particulars, so if a critic says, "Murray has mastered the black idiom," I'm proud of that. I would also be proud if somebody said I'd mastered French, Italian, Latin, or the stream-of-consciousness technique. I'm striving to be a representative twentieth-century American writer. *Black,* by the way, isn't even a term I [like to] use. I'm not black, I'm a shade of brown

[, which is not a shade of blackness]. *African American* is a term I don't understand. [It suggests official segregation as do social science survey categories.] I prefer *Negro* myself, but better still *colored people.* That's a fine term. It's ambiguous enough to denote us, because we're an ambiguous people. [And so are all other Americans. So why not just American? To me *colored* or *brownskin* suggests a functional description not unlike *brunette, blonde,* or *redhead.*

TS: But *Negro* is such an old-time racist expression.

AM: No it isn't. That's not true. Malcolm X and his bunch started that crap. Most other people were mainly concerned with having it capitalized and pronounced correctly. The word they rejected as racist was *Negress.* For a more scholarly account on the usage of the word *Negro,* see H. L. Mencken's *The American Language,* Supplement One.]

TS: What writer exemplifies the blues idiom?

AM: The attitude toward experience that Hemingway expresses strikes me as a literary equivalent to what I find in the blues. Let me put it this way: If you want to find the blues idiom in literature, don't read any so-called black writers; read Hemingway. These other guys, all they're talking about is justice and injustice. They ain't ever going to equal Hemingway, who's talking about life and death.

TS: What other artists?

AM: Bearden's approach to composition has the same spirit of improvisation you find in jazz. So do Calder's mobiles and stabiles.

TS: One might well ask, What on earth does Alexander Calder have in common with Count Basie?

AM: Basie could make one note swing, Calder could make one piece of metal swing. Look, what I'm trying to do is account for the sources of an adequate aesthetic for dealing with contemporary experience. I'm just trying to find an adequate form, and I haven't found one anywhere that does it better than what I call the blues idiom. Hemingway used bullfighting to work out an aesthetic for literature; I use jazz.

TS: And you have worked to make your writing style the verbal equivalent of jazz.

AM: Yes. I got the idea from reading Thomas Mann. Mann was of consuming interest to me; he was what really got me going. My Thomas Mann file dates back to 1938, when I had just become curious about writing and was studying literary devices. I read the preface to *The Magic Mountain,* where Mann talks about how he took the leitmotif method from Wagner. He was using music as a model. The idea appealed to me tremendously. Now, Mann's context was Bach, Beethoven, and Wagner. What was mine? I started checking through American music. One thing that did not do it for me was *Rhapsody in Blue.* So I thought, What's closest to me? And Luzana Cholly, the blues guitar player from *Train Whistle Guitar,* was one of the first characters I drew, in 1951. Here's what I said about writing fiction way back then: "We all learn from Mann, Joyce, Hemingway, Eliot and the rest, but I'm also trying to learn to write in terms of the tradition I grew up in, the Negro tradition of blues, stomps, ragtime, jumps and swing. After all, very few writers have done as much with American experience as Jelly Roll Morton, Count Basie and Duke Ellington."

TS: So you went all around the block, by way of Thomas Mann, to come back home.

AM: You'd never get where I got by just listening to a goddamn guitar player in a honky-tonk. You'd never write a novel. I had to come through novels, and there were no Negro novels that reached the level of sophistication I was reaching for. *The New Negro,* Alain Locke's anthology of the so-called Harlem Renaissance, was sandlot stuff compared with Eliot, Pound, Mann, [Proust,] and Joyce.

TS: Your fiction is largely the product of a long grappling with what you say are the four basic narrative categories. Can you explain your very particular understanding of tragedy, comedy, melodrama, and farce?

AM: In order to have a story, you have contention. You have a desire, a wish, but something's in the way. So you have agon—struggle. The one that carries the values we identify with, we call the protagonist. The one that threatens those values is the antagonist. One is indispensable to the other. No dragon, no hero.

Now, what are the interactions of this antagonism? When the protagonist is overcome, it's a tragedy. When he succeeds and he reaches a new perception of life and resolves his misunderstanding, it's a comedy. If you wipe out the dragon [as in medieval romance], that's melodrama. You have what the Greeks call a *deus ex machina,* the resolution of the antagonism through efficient engineering. It's like a Western, where the gunfighter comes into town and kills the bad guy as the swordsman once slew dragons. That's what social science literature does. All these poor people can't do such and such because they're poor, so you wipe out poverty [with welfare programs].

TS: And farce?

AM: Well, farce means you accept the fact that the whole shebang could come apart at any time—your universe, everything you know. Farce brings you closer to the point of view Hemingway expressed as "winner take nothing." You're back to entropy, back to the fact that life adds up to *nada,* to nothing.

TS: It sounds like modern consciousness.

AM: To me, farce is an expression of the truly contemporary sensibility. But a new kind of farce—what I called straight-faced farce. That's the Murray dimension. Most exemplars of the modern consciousness go after despair. But farce lets you face what Hemingway faced: that the winner shall take nothing. That ultimately it doesn't matter whether you succeed or fail. You're gonna die, man. There's a beautiful love affair, and the bride and groom are killed the next day. But you persist. [You regain such ever so tentative balance and perspective that you're able to come by. Farce represents slapstick behavior in slapdash predicaments.]

Now, here is where it all hooks up. To me, the blues idiom and farce are more or less synonymous. And they embrace all the categories. The blues idiom lets you deal with tragedy, comedy, melodrama, and farce in the same statement. Take a blues song. The lyrics are tragic. The lyrics tell a tale of woe. But the presentation counterstates that. The musicians are playing something full of life and joy and mockery; that's the comic aspect. The jazz musician is the questing hero of melodrama, who crafts a sword, his chops, his technique, to slay the dragon of the blues. But the entire blues statement is a farce, a recognition that you can establish order but it always reverts to chaos. The blues will be back tomorrow! [Slapdash. Slapstick. Charlie Chaplin behavior but not for vaudeville amusement. Straight-faced farce. Hey, man, what is Charlie Chaplin's behavior about if not elegance, his every move? Even his ridiculous sartorial getup is geared to elegance! Man, he doesn't just walk, he dances.]

TS: In *The Seven League Boots,* I miss a sense of struggle, of Scooter grappling with conflict, inner or outer. He has a pretty easy sail.

AM: Why do you say that? He doesn't yet know what he wants to do with himself. What's he accomplished?

TS: He's the bassist in the best jazz band in America.

AM: That's not his objective and why should he be in pain over that? [He has developed enough technique to express a sensibility that the band leader finds useable at this stage of the band's ongoing effort. He is not faked out by show biz lotus eaters, sirens, calypsos, or Circe, who turns out to be something of a fairy tale aunt. And besides, didn't *Train Whistle Guitar* and *The Spyglass Tree* make it clear enough that Scooter is not a person of fragile integrity?] You've come up in an age of bullshit psychology and psychiatrists, so you think everybody should be sick. I don't think so. I think the blues [response] is the answer. If you can swing and you've got your health you can get through things [substitute for "things": disjunctures and obstructions]. If you view the antagonist as cooperative, struggle becomes opportunity. Is the jazz soloist struggling or is he being creative? Why was Louis Armstrong always smiling? People have had to make something up. "He must have been suffering from *something* to create such art!" I didn't see it. I didn't see it in Duke. Did you see it in Duke?

TS: No, he had pretty smooth sailing.
AM: How about Basie?

TS: Smooth sailing.
AM: Went from one thing to another. Once a guy becomes successful, everybody accuses him of not having to struggle. It's like Negro basketball players. "Oh, he's a natural athlete."

TS: How can a reader identify with Scooter if everything is so easy for him?
AM: The reader can take him as an ideal. Now the reader's got someone he could aspire to be like. Scooter has to fail? Every genius failed before he succeeded? I don't think so.

TS: It might give the story some drama, some suspense.
AM: If that's what you're after, you can write a melodrama. See, a person with a conventional mind would be perfectly happy if the mob ran Scooter out of Hollywood because he's shacking up with a white woman. I wouldn't write a story like that. It would wreck the whole thing that I'm getting at, because it becomes civil rights. I'm not writing about civil rights. I'm writing about what happens to a talented—or at any rate, competent—person. If Thomas Mann can write about gifted people, why can't I? I really don't see that Scooter has it any easier than [James Joyce's] Stephen Dedalus.

TS: Stephen Dedalus sweats a whole lot more.

AM: He's a jig-cropping Irishman! He can't ["can't" replaced by the following: does not] swing [although Joyce does.]! You've got to tell some stories about some guys who can swing. I mean, that's a pretty square guy in *Invisible Man* by Ralph Ellison, who, incidentally, was my close friend and literary colleague and who knew exactly what he was doing—namely, writing a conventional Dostoyevsky-type novel. I'm not writing that kind of story. I'm writing about people I admire and identify with, like Duke Ellington. Is self-discipline a matter of suffering?

Scooter does what the protagonist of a farce does: He's trying to keep his balance and find himself. You want to drag me back into the old stuff. The guy's got to do this or that? No. He's having a hell of a time trying to find out what it is he's supposed to do. You see, you're looking for the same old story. I have a different perception of life. It's Cosmos Murray: Scooter and elegance versus entropy. My narrative structure is not geared to a tightly knit plot. It is a picaresque story, more a matter of one thing following another than one thing leading to another. To me, the "and then and then and also and also and next after that" of a picaresque reflects a sensitivity consistent with contemporary knowledge of the universe. The connection between that and the requirements of ongoing improvisation in the jam session should be easy to see.

TS: So the antagonist is entropy, nothingness, meaninglessness.

AM: Yes. And you don't have to think of it as evil. It's as impersonal as nature. Hemingway's bull is not evil. It's easy to go into sin versus righteousness, but if you start out with the conception of life as a farce, you're never really going to win.

TS: So what's the point then?

AM: What *is* the point of life? Nothing. It's just like grains of sand, except that we have human consciousness, so however many bars we have, we try to make them swing.

TS: The winner may take nothing, but he's still the winner.

AM: You're still clinging to a materialist conception that my work is against! Hemingway doesn't mean that. He means that what people are brought up to think is a prize is not a prize. You know the whole quotation, right? "The winner shall take nothing; neither his ease, nor his pleasure, nor any notions of glory; nor, if he win far enough, shall there be any reward within himself." No reward within himself! He doesn't even achieve a lasting equilibrium.

TS: But he wins. You're not going to tell me Hemingway wasn't a competitive SOB.

AM: You're confusing the writer with what he wrote. The man has to live up to everything he writes? That's what I tell people about Jefferson when they go on about him owning slaves. He put the basis for their freedom into the Declaration. Don't tell me about Thomas Jefferson owning slaves; he wrote the Declaration of Independence.

TS: So Scooter's life isn't about winning or losing.

AM: Just living, man. It's how many bars can you swing.

TS: That's a very, very sobering way of looking at life.

AM: You're goddamn right. It's about time, what with all those particles and waves and outer space and all the stuff we now know. When you're conscious of that, how can you cling to that other stuff? When you realize how precarious life is. This little chicken-shit star we're on, it ain't nothing, man. If you're going to live in terms of that, what the hell is evil? Somebody gets cancer nine months after he wins a million dollars. Did money help him? Is his disease a punishment for some trespass? I don't think so. So the problem is to find the way of accepting that it's a farce.

TS: Well, most people don't even get to the point where they perceive the nothingness, the absurdity. And if they do, they run from it as fast as they can by surrounding themselves with fictions, illusions, and comforts.

AM: Now you're getting to it. That's the point. Love is something you want to hold onto when you find it. Friendship. All these things. You've got emotions. You are capable of delight. But if you're sophisticated, you also go beyond that, because people are coming and going all the time. You see a guy at a funeral; he almost forgot about death. He should have known all the time it wasn't going to last forever. But you keep going. See, that's what Mann gets at in *The Magic Mountain*: I will never let death have sovereignty over my thoughts! That is the big moral of *The Magic Mountain*. In Mann, in Hemingway, you get beyond that lightweight stuff. The problems in Cosmos Faulkner are correctable, a matter of human fallibility. In Cosmos Hemingway the problems are inherent in the nature of things. Faulkner may have lots of complicated stuff going on [Perhaps not even Henry James was a greater master of convolution.], but Faulkner stops short of the void. Hemingway keeps going.

Albert Murray: Extensions and Elaborations

Roberta S. Maguire / 1996

This previously unpublished interview took place on July 26, 1996, and September 6, 1996, in Mr. Murray's apartment in Harlem. On the latter date, Miles Maguire was also present and joined in the conversation. Printed by permission of Roberta S. Maguire.

RM: When did you decide you wanted to write?

AM: In high school, I was more interested in drama, in acting and directing. When I was a college student, there's a book that I still have, *The Theatre: Three Thousand Years of Drama, Acting and Stagecraft,* by Sheldon Cheney, that was important for me. I think that's the first non-textbook that I bought with my own money. It gave me a comprehensive view of literature although I was concentrating on drama. It took me back into ritual, which is still discernible in my orientation to aesthetic statement. Also I had discovered anthropology. But the thing that gave me the strongest impulse to write was in my freshman composition class—I forget this from time to time—but I come back, it's there, it's a benchmark, you know—and you can see elaboration and extensions that as a freshman on a personal level I was engaged in and felt challenged to write. There was a piece by William Saroyan from *The Daring Young Man on the Flying Trapeze,* "Myself upon the Earth," that we were encouraged to use as a model to see if we could write about ourselves.

I was always considered a good storyteller, but I didn't connect that with writing. That came later. But when I was in college Hemingway was putting some things in *Esquire.* I had read some of Hemingway in high school and liked him, and read more in college. I thought, "I'd like to do that." So I turned from drama, playwriting, to prose.

RM: What did prose offer you that playwriting didn't?

AM: Poetry. I realized that prose could have a poetry that stage directions couldn't have. In prose, stage directions—setting the scene—became poetry. You do what Edna St. Vincent Millay does in her poem "Renascence": "All I could see from where I stood / Was three long mountains and a wood; / I turned and looked the other way, / And saw three islands in a bay." Then there's Hemingway's first paragraph of *To Have and Have Not:* "You know how it is there early in the morning in Havana with the bums still asleep against the walls of the buildings; before even the ice wagons come by with ice for the bars? Well, we came across the square from the dock to the Pearl of San Francisco Cafe to get coffee and there was only one beggar awake in the square and he was getting a drink out of the fountain. But when we got inside the cafe and sat down, there were the three of them waiting for us." When I was teaching, I would ask my students, "Did you see the palm trees?" He didn't even mention them, but with the rest of the description, you'd see them. I read Hemingway and thought, this is it. This is art.

RM: So how do you see the relationship between your nonfiction and your fiction? For example, Walker Percy, with whom you became friends in the late 1960s, early 1970s, saw them as very different things. He would turn from fiction to nonfiction when he was frustrated with a novel he was writing.

AM: Well, nonfiction is expository, so your problem is the logical or sequential arrangement of details. In fiction you are concerned with the psychological and chronological arrangement of details for the emotional impact an image makes. Most editors are going to look at your manuscript, fiction or otherwise, through Hemingway's glasses. When an artist does it, like Hemingway, it feels like it's reporting, but it's poetry. I realized this was the sort of thing I wanted to do and that would be my approach to language, but it's not a matter of only simplification because I had to deal with all that other stuff—the music in Joyce, and the complexity and convolution of James and Thomas Mann.

RM: And Faulkner.

AM: Yes. But when Faulkner really wants to put you there, he's got to rely on Hemingway's moves. Nobody beats Hemingway. Then you can get into some of that convolution that you're still trying to figure out. But the dust and so forth that you smell as well as see in *Light in August,* that's a Hemingway effect.

RM: I'll buy that. Since I brought up Faulkner and you brought up time and place, I want to ask whether you see yourself as a southern writer.

AM: Yes. The blues, all that stuff is southern. Jazz—that's really a southern export.

RM: So it's what you would say are the idiomatic particulars of the south that make you a southern writer—

AM: And an American writer. Because nothing else seduces as many Americans' sensibilities.

RM: In your mind, then, would it be accurate to say that the south is the most American region of the country, the place where everything that is American is most exaggerated, most obvious?

AM: Perhaps in some ways. But after all there's nothing more convention- ally American than midwesterners. They have the general unidiomatic type of demeanor that common garden variety have. Also they don't have the restrictions to the same extent that Americans elsewhere have. And they also seem more accessible. You don't get so much of that paranoid provincial stuff you get in the deep south. And southerners don't sound like the text- books. Midwesterners sound like the textbooks, sound like the dictionary. That's the way grade-school teachers sounded to me. "Miss Lexine Metcalf" sounded like a midwesterner because she would say "ing," etc., etc., and didn't slur any syllables.

RM: How would you characterize your relationship with whites when you were growing up?

AM: There was a sort of convention that you recognized when you came up in a segregated time. We didn't dislike white people. There was just a special etiquette that was involved in a relationship with some of them, given the circumstances. Of course with those hobo guys on the railroad coming by asking for food—we didn't have any reason to feel inferior to white peo- ple. Just because they put that status stuff out there didn't mean we were going to go along with it. We saw too many bony-butt poor white crackers. We were going to feel inferior to them? You see what I mean? We knew they were worse off than we were. They didn't look like they were getting as much to eat as the smart little colored kids. As southerners we didn't automatically dislike southern whites because there were too many people that were right there in your neighborhood and churches, etc., who looked just like them and who identified themselves as colored.

So the most exotic thing to me about white people was when they sounded like midwesterners. Because they sounded like a textbook. They sound like the girls should sound that you were looking at in the magazines. Because models don't look like they sound like any hillbilly girls. This was before Andie MacDowell, to be sure!

RM: I like how you define yourself as a southern writer by way of the blues and jazz, but you don't appear to be concerned about anybody else who is considered a southern writer. Folks will say, "No, I'm not a southern writer," with "southern writer" defined by Faulkner. But how do you see yourself in relation to those so-called Southern Renascence writers like Faulkner and Robert Penn Warren?

AM: Part of it. Part of my heritage, a most intimate part of my heritage. I certainly had to come to terms with Hemingway and then Faulkner in college. Faulkner—*Light in August.* That dust along the roadside. And in "Dry September." I'd ask myself, can you make that stuff live like that? And he was making it live more for me than T. S. Stribling and people like that. I was reading that too, which was also downhome stuff.

RM: It seemed everybody was.

AM: Erskine Caldwell's *God's Little Acre* was very popular at that time, and I also remember *Kneel to the Rising Sun,* Margaret Mitchell's *Gone with the Wind.* Hemingway was in *Esquire* and, after all, he was writing about the south, too. He was writing about Florida in *To Have and Have Not.*

RM: So you see yourself as a part of the southern literary tradition—adding on.

AM: Yes, without the special ideological stuff about agrarianism, of course. It's about aesthetic kinship, a concern with the nature of art as such.

In my last years of college I realized that what was especially interesting was aesthetics. As did the Agrarians, the Vanderbilt group with John Crowe Ransom. They were interested in it too. They were calling for close analysis.

RM: The New Criticism.

AM: Yes. Cleanth Brooks and Robert Penn Warren. *Southern Review* and *Sewanee Review,* those magazines were there at Tuskegee, and I was looking for definitions. I started that back in high school. I wanted to know what this stuff was. I wasn't going to jump up and go off with some ideology, some social program. I was interested in: What is art? What is literature? What is painting? What is a poem? You would write conventional academic definitions for an examination, but these guys, the New Critics, were not writing this for an assignment. This was practical, everyday stuff.

We had a big library at Tuskegee. We had all those literary magazines. *North American Review* was still being published at that time. The *Atlantic Monthly. Scribner's* went out by the time I got out of high school. I was reading the *Nation, New Republic,* the *Saturday Review of Literature,* and the quarterlies. I thought one day I would write essays like those that appeared there. So, back to your first question, my decision to write comes out of this.

RM: Since you became particularly interested in aesthetics in college because you wanted to know what art was, did that lead you to read aestheticians, semioticians like Susanne Langer? How did you get to her?

AM: That happened many years later. I discovered Susanne Langer when my first story was published in *New World Writing.* She had a piece in it. I had known about her. But that's why I started reading her. I knew about her work regarding art and sentience.

RM: Was it that she was articulating something that you were coming to understand yourself?

AM: I had read all kinds of stuff by this time. Since I was interested in aesthetics I had known about Langer's book *Feeling and Form.* And then I read *Philosophy in a New Key* and also *Problems of Art: Ten Philosophical Lectures.* Look at what she's saying: Everything is feeling with her. And that's what art is about: What it connotes is more important than what it denotes.

RM: So if everything is feeling with her, is it fair to say that everything is feeling with you?

AM: I would agree with her that art represents the life of human feeling—how it feels to be human. See, what you're really doing is stylizing an experience. That's why she says sentience—feeling—right? Your consciousness of your feeling. Now art makes us aware of that on a certain level. It enhances—life. We live things over and we have what we call vicarious experience. All that comes together in her approach to art.

RM: You already had written part of *Train Whistle Guitar* when you came across her ideas. So clearly that's what you were thinking anyhow.

AM: Right. I was vulnerable to it. I was open to that type of thinking because of what I had come to see. I probably got it from Thomas Mann and his ideas regarding the nature of expression. And also there was what I had picked up about fiction from those letters that Hemingway was writing to *Esquire* magazine while I was in college.

RM: Certainly that accounts for the texture of your writing, and when you make the move in your books, as in *Seven League Boots,* or in any of the novels—"and that's when she said what she said about"—this seems to me to be related to Langer's and your ideas about sentience.

AM: I think so. She's got a lot of it, but it can't tell you everything. But you don't need it to tell you everything. You come to a point when you're writing and you say, "Do I define it or do I project it?" That's exactly where I am right now in the chapter I'm working on. It's like musical figures. Like the opening of *Train Whistle Guitar.* The first paragraph? I don't see how I can say it better than that. That paragraph is a poem really, you see? You can't say all of what's going on at the moment. Otherwise you'd be laying on so many details you'd be rivaling Dostoyevsky, laying on the details and explaining rather than evoking with images, movement, and pulse. As great as Dostoyevsky is considered to be, that's not what my taste leads me to try to do in fiction.

RM: So you compress feeling to an art symbol.

AM: Right. Appropriate to the work, just as a poem does, just as imagery does. You have two poetic devices—devices of sound, devices of imagery. And imagination. So you can suggest the ineffable with sound and somehow you know what's being described. So you've got something that is a symbol of something else, which you hope is a symbol of a lot of other things.

RM: What you've got, then, is a scholastic idea, something being present in another form of existence.

AM: Right. Right. Art is always concerned with that. You see? That's what the image is. You've got those two different functions of language: the denotative function and the connotative function. Then you can narrow it down—and channel it. You know, getting your clothes out of the laundry, getting your assignments in, meeting new people, writing letters home—that's the also and also that captures that first semester of college. You can go on and on with those long Dostoyevsky paragraphs of explanation and analysis, and you forget what the damn story is from time to time. On the other hand, the discursiveness in Thomas Mann's *Magic Mountain* and *Joseph and His Brothers* doesn't bother me.

RM: Walker Percy said that the secret hope in the back of the mind of every novelist is that he's going to make an ultimate discovery in a novel. Some ultimate truth is going to become clear. Do you agree?

AM: I think I could go along with that. I mean, sometimes you know what it is. Sometimes you don't realize all the implications of what it is. It is the nature of metaphor that when you write and then you come back to it, *you* learn something new from it too—perhaps it's like becoming aware of overtones that are more a matter of dimension than deliberation.

So you've read all of my stuff now? You've read *Seven League Boots?*

RM: Yes I have.

AM: All right. What's the book about? It's about American identity. What are all of my books about? "Myself upon the Earth." Yourself upon the earth. Themselves upon the earth. Right?

Why did I invent the Marquis de Chaumienne? To have an objective take on American identity. Why does Jewel Templeton take up with Scooter? She went over to St. Moritz and found out she didn't know what it meant to be an American. And this guy's telling her, "You and Daisy Miller and Bessie Smith." And she thinks, "What is this?" [Chuckles.] Daisy Miller OK. But Bessie Smith?

RM: *Seven League Boots* is my favorite of your novels—maybe it's because it's the most recent one that I've read—but I found the Marquis and Jewel Templeton kind of scary characters.

AM: Why?

RM: Well, as you intended, I didn't think Jewel Templeton had any concept of who she was, which came across as dangerous.

AM: Perhaps none or only a few of those Hollywood girls know what their work adds up to. But the ambition to be and do something significant brings this into focus for Jewel. See what I mean? This is intended to be a real all-American novel! They keep trying to push me into civil rights—this represents a bigger ambition than that.

RM: I thought both the Marquis and Templeton were dangerous for Scooter and was glad that he didn't get caught up in their stuff.

AM: Well, that's what the guy missed who said, "Where's the tension in the book?" But that's the point. I mean, when I was working on the book, for years, I called that section of it (the Jewel Templeton section) "one thousand plus one"—a thousand and one nights. And then I decided to bring the focus back to identity: Apprenticeship—journeymanship—craftsmanship. What Scooter's got to do at this juncture is resist temptation. That's where some of the tension is. Like the idea in the *Odyssey* is to get home. Right? So you've got a lot of attractive obstacles, like Calypso, the Sirens, Circe. Circe turns out to be a guide. She turns other guys into swine, but she's the one who says, "You got to go this way, then this way." She sends them to Hades and all that—"You got to go through that before you can go back." Circe turns out to be an indispensable part of him getting back home. He says, "I got to go." She says, "OK, I'll help you, but you know, you gotta go this way, then you go this way, then you go that way."

RM: So, translated to *Seven League Boots,* you gotta go to Paris.

AM: It's not literally that. Paris is not really Hades, although Paris is a place where one spends much time communing with the great spirits of other times who do enhance your return home. But the convention of the guide remains, which is ironic because they both, Jewel and Scooter, see themselves as being proteges of the other. Jewel comes to learn about the significance of jazz from this very sophisticated European who sees it as essential to a definition of American culture and American character. So when she comes back to the U.S., she's very careful about how she chooses Scooter; she looks very carefully at these guys, these musicians, before she makes her choice. It's not a matter of her finding Scooter irresistible or something like that—that's not what the book is about. And it's not a big deal for a professional jazz musician to get a date with a movie star. With a jazz band like *that* jazz band? *They're going to line up!* When Duke [Ellington] sent for me to come out to Coconut Grove, after the show, backstage the people lining up were mostly movie stars—come backstage to see the musicians and their friends! It wasn't any big deal at all for the musicians in a band like that or musicians headlining in any significant spots out that way.

RM: Jewel Templeton, then, she's reasonably older than Scooter.

AM: Right.

RM: Scooter, all the time in your books, is involved with older women. How come?

AM: It's a matter of *rite de passage*. He's got to be prepared for the younger one. The only way he can do that is to get it from the gettin' place. You've got to have a good fairy godmother. They're all teachers for him. Another dimension of Athena and Telemachus.

RM: He had a lot of teachers.

AM: That's why he can get along. There's nothing wild about this guy. No unnecessary chances—that's too much. He just has one life. He's just hanging by a thread. So if he's not going to be careful with himself, how's he going to be careful with anything else? Why should he live, if he can't make himself live and do as well by himself as he can? That's what I think. I'm not going to take anything that's going to mess me up. I'm going to take dope? You gonna miss something really good if you get hung up with that fake stuff.

RM: I think that the most intense relationship with an older woman that Scooter has is with Hortense Hightower at the end of *Spyglass Tree*.

AM: And there's no sex in that.

RM: No, but that's what I was sure was going to happen until she gives him the bass fiddle. It was building to a very nice climax there and then he gets an instrument.

AM: Yes, when he runs into Will Spradley.

RM: Yes, but when he first arrives at Hortense Hightower's that afternoon, I thought, I know what's going on, I've read enough of this book. But then there's Will Spradley. Yet there's still that moment at the end when she says to Scooter, "I've got something for you." And she had the bass fiddle.

AM: All of this is consistent with her conception of his orientation to music and also to life. She didn't want him to miss hearing anything, so he could listen better with a bass fiddle. Because he's a timekeeper. But remember the woman who picks Scooter up at that party; she sees the fiddle as a woman, she makes that big buxom Gaston Lachaise image synonymous with the instrument. So you've got that snuck in. She's the perfect person to put that in.

RM: But Scooter got warned away from her.

AM: Oh yes, the other guys told Scooter, "You gotta be careful about that one." Fay Morgan, Fata Morgana! *Femme fatale!*

RM: My favorite woman in *Seven League Boots* is Gaynelle Whitlow.

AM: [Laughs.] She is often the favorite of a lot of readers of all persuasions. There was a woman in the Madison Avenue book store who said, "I want to be her friend so I can taste that sweet potato pie!"

RM: You know, she strikes me as being in the same mold as Deljean McCray.

AM: Yes.

RM: Now, do you see her as a blues hero as well?

AM: Yes, she's about the intrinsic meanings aside from material achievement or publicity. She's a fine woman. The person in tandem in the overall Scooter cycle with her is Creola Calloway. She and Creola have a similar perspective: "I don't have to achieve anything, get a newspaper personality, be a star, to have a life." That's how they answer the question, "What is life about?," which is a basic existential question. All these other people, they have an inscription for Creola's tombstone all ready: *"She could have been famous."* That didn't mean anything to her. So that's why Gaynelle tells her rich date, "I don't want to be mistaken for a movie star. I just want them to think I'm your secretary and I'm out with the Bossman." She says, "I read all those movie magazines. I like the way they *live* out here. I don't like that stuff that they're *doing* in their studios—all that hype is just to sell theatre tickets."

RM: So she doesn't have a very high opinion of the Jewel Templetons of the world.

AM: She's also just kidding. A good old downhome colored girl is always going to pull your leg about dating a white girl. So this is an inside kind of thing.

RM: You've said before that your ideas about American culture are extensions of ideas put forth by Constance Rourke and John Kouwenhoven. The latter especially talks about the interaction of the vernacular with learned cultures, that there is always cross-fertilization.

AM: The dynamics of cultural development and definition that emerge in Constance Rourke's work she inherited from some ideas of Johann von Herder, who articulated an approach to defining a given culture. Herder put her on to the idea that cultures begin on what I would call the folk level and develop upwards, whereas when people like Van Wyck Brooks were talking about the pilgrimage of Henry James and the ordeal of Mark Twain, they were talking about the absence of high culture in America, lamenting the lack. So what came out of Herder was this other natural history of a fine art, of a high art, of a given culture. It's all extension, elaboration, and refinement of the vernacular into a higher level.

In my thinking, culture can be separated into three levels, folk—pop—fine, and the last is where the masterpieces come; that's the ultimate definition of a culture, where stylization comes in. For example, you look at a picture and then make a painting, but the painting is not a report on the picture, because an artist is looking at it and seeing a type of design—a design statement or composition statement—that takes you to another realm. Once there, you get into nonfigurative painting. That's why the Cezanne show is so important to have right now, because he went right on out of figurative painting. You can go to Picasso and Braque, but Cezanne was already there. It's just like Louis Armstrong and jazz: You've got these other guys doing stuff, but Louis Armstrong was already there. And he, like Ellington, is a definitive example of American culture. He fulfills the vernacular imperative of processing idiomatic material into fine art by using indigenous devices.

RM: Well, then, how do you account for a phenomenon like Norman Rockwell?

AM: With photography coming in, the ultimate of that was Norman Rockwell! We do still have that weakness for Norman Rockwell, which is the *Saturday Evening Post* cover. You see, that's all-American—all pop American. When he finally did that famous thing on school desegregation, that was a very important imprimatur. Do you remember that? There are these two guys—U.S. marshals—taking the little brownskin girl to school. And once you've got school desegregation rendered in a Norman Rockwell, it's as all-American as July 4th. It's right up there with being tow-headed and freckle-faced!

What my stuff does is show that there's a brown-skinned one who is just as omni-American as the other. And elsewhere, probably even more, because if you go over there to Europe looking tow-headed and freckle-faced, you'll look like one of them: you could be a Dutch boy, you could be a German. But if you look like Duke Ellington or Count Basie, well, you're American. Surely not African, not to Europeans. Everything special about you is something made in America—made in the USA, as Langston Hughes once said on a Folkways record.

RM: Related to your notions regarding folk, pop, and fine art is a question I have about your relationship to the literary Harlem Renaissance. I know that you've said before that when you were a young man, you saw the writing of the Harlem Renaissance as limited, but yet what you say about those levels of art does remind me of what Alain Locke says in the introduction to *The New Negro* about looking to the folk and then refining folk culture to fine art. Where do you part ways with Locke?

AM: I didn't study that too seriously because I didn't find any of those writers to be at the depth that I required at the time. They were so preoccupied with being a Negro and all that sort of thing. It didn't cut from the political implications to a basis of aesthetics. See, none of these guys do that. Ralph Ellison and I were the first to try to do so. I wanted to make the best possible all-American. You could be anything. Those guys from the Harlem Renais-

sance on up are defining themselves as colored guys trying to get permission
to become American. But the cultural dynamics go beyond that. Even so, I
think the biggest difference is that they end up still asking for acceptance,
inclusion, whereas Ralph and I were interested in changing perceptions, saying, "*This* is it! This is American too, basic American!" All those white guys
in Chicago, the white musicians, going to hear downhome music, they were
breaking their largely imported conventions and coming out of their neigh-
borhoods and coming southside, saying, "This is what I want to sound like."
And they were doing that in the face of what the Ku Klux Klan was doing in
the south. But the dynamics were working, even while there was such preju-
dice that would make these guys say that Benny Goodman was the king of
swing; he could never approach Earl Hines, let alone Count Basie or Duke
Ellington. But the white guys are already contaminated, because they're playing Negro music! They're not playing Jewish music or Irish music—they're
playing Negro American music! No jazz musician wants you to say, "He
sounds like a white guy." He wants to sound as if to the idiom born!

But when you get down to the testimony, when you get down to the blues,
the idiomatic requirements are so profound and so subtle that getting those
timbres and those vibratos that have to go with it has got to be a cultural
enclave. No African can sing the blues. Most West Indians don't sing the
blues. So we are not talking about race. We are talking about idiom. If you
can't sound like a brownskin American from downhome, you can't sing the
blues.

RM: You have to have been in the Amen corner, right?

AM: That's right. If you've been in that, then you know where this stuff
is coming from. You got a secularized version, you know, of the call-and-
response, for example. You might see some really fine, technically fine, Danish musician in a Danish orchestra playing a solo in which he's really
"preaching a sermon." [Murray mimics playing the sax.] This Viking up
there with a saxophone sounding like that is quite a sight to behold!

Americans confuse culture and race, so idiomatic nuance is something that
is beyond them—they just say it's race. Now, if it's race, then West Indians
ought to be able to do it. They come from Africa. I have never seen them
swing without having picked it up stateside. Syncopation? Brownskin stateside vernacular.

RM: But you talk about how the drum beat that is so prevalent in the
blues, in jazz, has African origins.

AM: But that's just a disposition. It's a very important point of what I'm saying. The change in our music, the definitive influence that the African captives had on American music, was a *disposition* towards dance-oriented music, and the main feature of that was that it was percussive. But the Africans did not bring over music. There wasn't anybody to play their music for. This guy was from this tribe, that guy was from that tribe over here; they just might kill each other for trying to impose his own stuff. It could be like some snake charmer going into a synagogue. Or a Baptist going into a synagogue with pork chops—or pig's feet [laughs], or chitlins. Could you imagine that? It's the same thing with getting African cultures mixed up. So you see, they were not communicating anything that was African. Although they were communicating in a percussive manner, they had to communicate what was over here. Essentially, they were becoming Americans before anybody else simply because everybody else still had something from the old country to live in terms of. See, that's very fascinating stuff, and that's what we ought to have this generation be ready to come to terms with. The people freest to make an all-American synthesis were those who ironically are thought of as being the most ignorant. It simply meant that they were coming with less baggage. It's what Kouwenhoven points up: the interaction of the learned traditions and the frontier in the context of free enterprise. By free enterprise we simply mean experimental disposition: how do we adjust to this? This whole business of adaptation to the frontier is what's important. So you can't come over and build viaducts and aqueducts because you don't have the materials. But you can build trestles, because you've got a lot of trees. It's that type of thing.

Then look at what was to be done with all that coal and iron ore. Look at all of the U.S. engineering and architecture that came from the "I" beam!

RM: Could we go back to the Amen Corner for a second? Remember in that *Callaloo* piece, that conversation with you, Romare Bearden, James Baldwin, and Alvin Ailey, you and Baldwin in particular were talking about coming to terms with religion and the church. You were saying that while you were in Europe you needed to come to terms with the fact that the church could be the main vehicle of culture that you used for fine art. In reading that, I got some sense of ambivalence on your part about religion. In the Murray household, when you were growing up, how important was the church?

AM: I think the emotional response is in *Train Whistle Guitar.* So far as

an autobiography is concerned, I don't have any plans for doing what's in
them because the essentials involved with my coming to terms with my experience is in stylizing it into aesthetic statement. So the real truth of my attitude
toward formal religion is in the book. There you see Scooter looking at these
people and seeing them so weak and crying and going on and seeing the
stylized involvement that they had through the shouting—

RM: Miss Sister Lucinda Wiggins—

AM: Miss Sister Lucinda Wiggins [laughs]. Scooter knew where the hypocrisy was. He's a sharp guy, Scooter. He saw all these things. And then of
course all that stuff about his own history hit him. You know, everybody has
lied to Scooter. Mama is a saint. But she had lied about Miss Tee. That's very
complicated stuff. But even after he finds out the truth, he did not change
how he thought about Mama, and I haven't to this day: that's what a mama
is, what Mrs. Murray was. It didn't change anything, this shocking discovery;
Mama was still mama. I realized somehow that it was a part of the ritual of
growing up. You have that dynamic where the curtain is pulled back and you
are dis-illusioned. Like the illusion with Santa Claus. I did just what I did
about Santa Claus. I didn't let them know that I knew until circumstances
called for it. Actually, I never discussed it with the Murrays. I absolutely
could never do it.

RM: It strikes me that there are some interesting parallels between you
and Walker Percy, since you both spent formative years with people who
were not your biological parents. For Percy, his response to his personal
history undergirded everything he wrote. How about for you?

AM: It didn't seem to me that I had an abnormal childhood. My emotional
relationship to these other people really didn't change once it was revealed
that the Murrays were not my actual parents. Did you ever see Mrs. Murray's
picture? Here she is. And look at this: Doesn't that look like Faulkner?

RM: Yes.
AM: That's Mr. Murray.

RM: It could be Faulkner's brother.
AM: So, you see, how could I ever have any particular thing about some
white person. I have never seen anybody whiter than that. It seemed perfectly
natural to me to be involved with both lighter and darker skinned people.
Here's a picture of Miss Tee. You can see the resemblance. Sudie Graham
Burke was her name. I always addressed her as Auntie.

RM: Did you know her all your years growing up?

AM: Always. She was right there all the time. I couldn't figure it out. People were whispering, right? People gossiping about all kinds of stuff. Kids would always say something in a way that made you mad, so you would reject what they were saying, "Oh, he ain't your papa. Miss Sudie Burke your mama"—something like that. The kid that said that didn't like me anyway. He was always making fun of somebody. So it didn't have any impact. It *was* a problem at some point just as it is in *Train Whistle* with Miss Tee's husband. He could never get over the fact that she had a child before they married. He was very pretentious, an all but illiterate, ambitious type of guy, but he was a good provider. For me there would always be special things from Miss Sudie at Christmas time. But of course that would be precisely what a good fairy godmother would do.

Have you seen a picture of my actual father?

RM: No. When did you get to know him?

AM: My senior year in high school. I had never said anything to anyone that indicated I knew more about my beginnings than I had been told, but the way I finally communicated it to Sudie was when, in my senior year, I was on my way up to Tuskegee as the captain of the basketball team to play in the Southeastern high school basketball tournament. All that stuff between that time and the wake when I overheard what I did I'd never really discussed with her. But when I was going up there for the first time I assumed I had some relatives in Tuskegee. So I went by her house, said I was going to Tuskegee and asked if there was somebody she wanted me to meet. So she said, "I'll write you a letter." And she wrote me a letter, and she said, "I want you to go to Mrs. Lottie Green." Mrs. Lottie Green was part of a well-established family in Tuskegee. Her husband had been one of Booker Washington's real estate specialists when they were buying up those plantations as they expanded. Tuskeegeans were real downhome folks, they loved to own property. So Tuskegee is a town of beautiful homes—a real high standard of living compared with much of the south. Like Atlanta. You know Atlanta?

RM: Some.

AM: You know where the Negroes are in Atlanta? The Cascades and all those showplace pads? Well, Atlanta is a city of beautiful homes anyway. That was already the way it was long before all of the civil rights improvement of recent years.

So what had happened was that Sudie had come in from the country, and this must have been, oh, about 1915. Everybody worked at Tuskegee. You could work your way through college, get a job with somebody on the business staff. Sudie was working for Lottie Green. One of Mrs. Green's nephews was playing around with girls who were going to school. He seduced Sudie, and so she had to leave. She went down to Escambia County, to Nokomis, because there was a relative there who was teaching school. In Nokomis she gave the baby away. Then because of the expansion of war industries, she came to the Mobile area. She moved there when the Murrays moved into the Mobile area from a farming area. Mobile was a seaport town, and with the fall-out from industrial growth related to the war, other small towns on the outskirts benefitted. There was Chickasaw, which is where the Liberty ships were built. So people started moving from farming areas into the outskirts of Mobile where another and better paying type of employment was possible.

When I was a high school senior, Sudie gave me this letter, and I took it to Lottie Green, and she told me where to find John. He was at the power plant. He was the boiler room foreman, the boiler room engineer. As I mentioned to you, Tuskegee was like a city-state in that it was almost self-sufficient: It had its own power plant, so it could produce its own light and power and ice, water, and whatnot. They had their own laundry. All of that continued until well after I became an instructor there, when they finally hooked into the Alabama power company. So it was a heck of a place. Anyhow, by that time, John was married and had a daughter who was eleven who was delighted to have an older brother. And after my freshman year of college, he made a basement apartment for me at his house, two rooms.

The essentials—what my personal history means to me—is contained in what I've written about it. The essential truth of it, the emotional impact, I've dealt with there, like the scene where Scooter comes home to show Miss Tee his report card, and she looks at it and says, "Don't you think Miss Melba [Mama] ought to see this first?" A flat report won't do it any better, aside from giving actual names and actual people. But then I've made composites out of them.

But if I could return to your question about religion for a moment: the church in my town was Hopewell Baptist Church, which I changed to Good Hope. It was near the car line. And the requirements were quite stringent. But what impressed me the most was how Sunday morning was so quiet. There were levels of that quiet, which you get in Duke Ellington's "Come Sunday." Do you know that?

RM: I don't know that.

AM: Do you remember the Sunday morning part of *Train Whistle Guitar?*

RM: Yes, I do.

AM: OK, let's get *Black, Brown, and Beige.* [Plays a few excerpts.] This is "Work Song," so this is during the week. And now it's Sunday morning—what you notice is how the plucking suggests the church bells in the distance. Can't get more prayerful than that. Now you hear the church organ. This is the stylization of the downhome voice from church, right? Multiplied by 15.

RM: I'm ready to go to that church.

AM: That can be paired, in *Train Whistle,* with the part about the ice in the ice bucket. So in *Train Whistle* there is a literary statement about Sunday morning in the same sense that Ellington's is a musical statement. That's how all this involvement with jazz works in my book. That quietness you heard is in the first paragraph. And there are train whistles in the other chapters. But when you get away from the locomotive onomatopoeia into this quiet stuff, with the food, the perfumes, or just some sweetheart soap in those days, you have extension, elaboration, and refinement.

RM: You did a nice match.

AM: That's the challenge. And that's from Thomas Mann. How did he get Bach and Wagner and so forth into *The Magic Mountain,* into the *Joseph* stories? You've got the abstract dynamics of the natural history, but then you've got to get your own idiomatic particulars, you see, and then it's the amount of technological sophistication you bring to that, plus what your mind is—the context that your mind occupies: Joyce, Mann, Faulkner, Kafka, anybody. How do you get Dylan Thomas in, you know what I mean? You know, you go out after *Christmas in Wales?* You going to put Alain Locke's choice of fiction up there against that stuff? That's some rough stuff. [Laughs.] You're not going to be the literary equivalent of Michael Jordan if the selections in *The New Negro* anthology represent the level of your game. They changed the rules of basketball for the Negroes, right? These guys came up and were so good that they had to re-invent, re-engineer, and re-manufacture the backboard so that they could slam-dunk. They re-made the whole thing.

MM: What position did you play when you played basketball?

AM: It was a totally different game. I played forward. The taller guys were the guards. In those days the average and smaller guys were assumed to have more maneuverability when dribbling. We would get the ball and bring it back up. So the tall guys are there to get the ball and give it to the average or even little guys, who would get it back up court. When they allowed the slam-dunk, it completely wiped out what used to be the crip shot. The crip shot was a hop-step and then you made a leap, and you spun the ball off the backboard. It was a close-range shot. They don't do that any more. They do it all in one motion now. That choreography redesigned much of the game. Many times the refinement in the culture comes from the so-called culturally deprived. So you see, if you approach the dynamics of a culture as natural history, it's like you're a good mechanic: "This is connected to that, and this goes with this, which comes from over here," etc.

I try to keep culture debates away from injustice, status, and exploitation—that's not the way to study it. Dynamics is dynamics, fair or foul.

RM: In *Blue Devils of Nada,* you discuss the writer's responsibility to respond to the cultural conditions of the moment. One point in particular struck me in that discussion: You argue that the one philosophical question we all are faced with is whether one should commit suicide.

AM: [Laughs.] Right. That's Camus. It's also Shakespeare, "To be or not to be." See the vamp to *Stomping the Blues.*

RM: So, clearly, then, that's something that you're looking at in your books: What is the point of going on, of continuing to live. Do you think that this question is more urgent at this point in the twentieth century, our postmodern era, than it was, say, at the end of the nineteenth century? Or do you see the existential condition as having been the same for the last century or two?

AM: I think there are two ways of looking at that. One is that you have to deal with whatever is there in your time. If you get involved in comparisons, you could get entrapped in things that might not be relevant for making comparisons regardless of what the comparisons are. They're not going to be the same. This is not the Middle Ages. They achieved what Lewis Mumford at some point called the Medieval Synthesis—that was when the average person in medieval Europe knew the meaning of life, knew why he was born, knew what he had to do to have a good life, knew what would happen when he was dead. He knew what the sky was. In other words, he didn't, but he did. He responded to that and so the bishops and other persons of authority could explain anything: "If you do this, you transgress. If you do this, your soul will go to heaven." And they really thought that they were going to have blue, brown, or green eyes and they would be blond, brunette, or red heads when they got into heaven—not that they ever really *said* that. And I'm sure some guys thought they were going to be slimmer or taller or shorter or something when they got to heaven. They couldn't visualize things otherwise. Well, there were those angelic wings, to be sure. Personification can really mess up your sense of the physical actualities of the universe! All these things are both a curse and a blessing. So I think that sometimes when you get into historical issues, historical configurations, and you make comparisons of this configuration with that, there might be some lessons that you could get, but it also might throw you off from coming to terms as best you can with what you have to face.

That brings you back to that basic thing that I borrowed from Kenneth Burke—about frames of acceptance and frames of rejection. Frames of rejection lead you to plaint, complaint, lament, elegies, satire, all that. Protest, outcry. Frames of acceptance mean you've got to go out and forge a sword. You've got to make what in the military we call an estimate of the situation, and it should be accurate. Then you figure out what the ammunition will be, what the force will be. You're so busy trying to figure out what is this and how do we deal with it that you can't go into a lament: It wasn't like this a hundred years ago. Instead of lamentation you have pep rallies. And when you win you get to celebrate. It's the frame of acceptance that leads to paens, odes, and epics!

RM: When you're talking about Burke and his frames of acceptance and frames of rejection, it reminds me of something you were saying in the interview with Tony Scherman that appeared in *American Heritage*. He was asking you to explain your ideas about narrative categories—tragedy, comedy, and farce in particular. In response, you mentioned that your concept of the straight-faced farce is what the Scooter books basically illustrate. From that I extrapolate that the farce is the appropriate response to the existential condition—

AM: —and is consistent with improvisation. And you don't know where this guy is going. Like in jazz, you're out there soloing and you hit a clinker, and Duke likes it and he hits it, so you've got to play it again. He picks it up immediately. Now you're playing in tandem. Somebody sets a riff behind that, and you're out there doing it. If you want to make a political extrapolation on that, then you come back to the United States, you see? You got it right there. Where do you end up? With Ellington and the Constitution.

You're going to junk the Constitution? You're *not* going to junk the *Constitution.* You elect the right guys. You don't go out moaning like the people who lost the O. J. Simpson case, who want to change the whole system. Their attitude is similar to that of the Republicans who, after they had Roosevelt, wanted to limit presidential service to two terms. They never figured on Reagan, whom they could have had in there for three terms. [Laughs.] Came back to haunt them.

RM: If we stick with those categories that you set up for literature, where would you put Faulkner?

AM: His content is tragedy—classically tragic, the Fall of the House of Atreus. There was an ancestral curse; there was an ancestral sin. And when he gets through with it, everybody's involved with it: "The land was not his to sell, and a person cannot hold another person as property." The Indians are just as guilty as everybody else, ultimately, to Ike McCaslin, right? Did I mention a terrific essay on Faulkner? It's called "The Figural Action of *Go Down, Moses.*" Here's the first paragraph: "Faulkner's *Go Down, Moses* is so patently a collection of short stories written at different times in the author's career that some audacity and no little faith are required to maintain its unity as a composition. Even when we accept Faulkner's own testimony that the work is a novel, we still have the problem of how to approach this assemblage of loosely related stories with no apparent central character or plot. An obvious precedent is available, one as familiar to the reader as to Faulkner: the Bible. Why have the clues not been taken more seriously? The title of the work, the names of the characters, the parallelling of incidents, the essentially eschatological outlook? Faulkner's imagination was steeped, as he himself admitted, 'in the best of all stories.' " The Bible! She's talking about a real problem of American identity. And you get this in "The Bear," this sense of the problem of brotherhood, when you come back to Sam Fathers. Sam had three brothers—Indian, white, and black. So the whole thing is a struggle to establish the appropriate brotherhood in the American context. And what's getting in the way is race. Isn't that terrific? There it is right there. You get Sam Fathers who has three brothers, you've got Ike McCaslin, you've got Tomey's Terrell: they're all messed up. And you've got Lucas Beauchamp who's got the strongest dose of the aristocratic strain in the Edmonds family.

RM: Yes, he does.

AM: Remember when they go to the store and Lucas steps aside and lets

Edmonds go in, not in deference, but because he was more familiar with the
venue. He'd been there before. In *Intruder in the Dust,* he says, "They know
I wouldn't shoot him in the back. They know me better than that." He makes
it clear that they've got to take on the responsibility of proving him innocent.
He has so much disdain for the guy. He's not going to say "I'm innocent"
because, he's thinking, "You should know I'm innocent." So Faulkner's
playing these wild jokes: Where is the nobility? Where is the nobility in *The
Sound and the Fury?* Where is the humanity in *The Sound and the Fury?*

RM: In Dilsey.

AM: Who represents the possibility of redemption. You see? Sin and redemption. The possibility of deliverance from the ancestral curse! Well, if
you read Faulkner, and if you believe it, and it really has an impact on you,
it can be a part of your personal literary dimension. Why not me? you can
ask. As Miss Lexine Metcalf in *Train Whistle Guitar* says, "Who if not you?"
You know that Quentin can't measure up, you know that Caddy doesn't measure up, you know that Jason doesn't measure up. So the source of it just
might be Lucas and *those* brownskin kinfolks. Since they had the hardest
time getting education, they might do the most with it. [Laughs.] How many
Jesus Christs do you need? How many Beowulfs? How many Seigfrieds?
That's why I hate sociology. Sociologists would say, "But he's an exception." That's what an epic is about, the exceptional person, the hero.

RM: That's a good point.

AM: With a farce, it is ultimately geared to entropy. Whether you know it
or not, life is going to be about a bunch of particles and waves. When you go
back into the Middle Ages, they didn't promise you particles and waves, they
just said "soul"—your soul will stay alive. But if you put the particles and
waves under certain environmental conditions, you might be Albert Murray.

RM: All right, let's take Walker Percy, then, and put him into your narrative scheme. Is he writing straight-faced farce as well?

AM: He may not have been as aware of it.

RM: But I think maybe he was.

AM: I think however you define it—well, there's a kinship, although a
different frame of reference, so that he formulates it in a different way. But
there's a kinship of sensibilities.

RM: I do think that there is a kinship of sensibility between you and Percy.

AM: Yes, but because of his background he's still influenced by his training in medicine and the sciences—positivism, materialism, and whatnot. Basically, underneath there's probably the desire on Percy's part to arrive at a mathematical proof. If this is true, there probably could be . . . do you see what I mean?

RM: Absolutely. One sees that with his insistence on a new scientific empiricism to get at an understanding of the use of language.

AM: But also, what are we to make of his conversion to formal religion? So the intellectual sensibility is slightly different. But when the actual experience hits you, the kinship is evident and we say "Amen." We understand that the kinship may be on different levels. I think if we understand those differences, they function in an ecumenical fashion. So we get back to what Joyce says, "Oystrygods gagging fishygods." In *South to a Very Old Place,* the second vamp, there's this paragraph where it talks about those razor-back crackers and those squint-eyed guys looking like downhome folks. He's on his way to New Haven. So the outchorus for that is: "Yes alas and alas, the also and also of all them and that of all that, plus much more; and furthermore 'what clashes here of wills gen wonts,' which is to say shaggy heads versus woolly heads much the same, alas, as if they were still 'oystrygods gagging fishygods' "—there's Joyce—"has never been any less familiar than all the rest and best of it."

Oystrygods gagging fishygods—shaggy heads versus woolly heads. There's always going to be some reason for somebody to clash. If you can't accept that, forget it. What was going on in Joyce's thing was: How can we possibly deal with those people—they eat fish, with scales on them! Whereas the other group says, "They're not human! They eat these things with these ugly shells, and they've got to break them on rocks. They're not human!" That for me is very important. I think about that all the time when I think about conflict. That's a universal element in human nature. And that connects with "which goes to show that the most natural state of human existence is a low grade of savagery."

RM: Who said that?

AM: That was Lord Raglan on the hero. He continues: "From whence comes the promise of the arts. But for the arts we're still at a primitive level of civilization." All that law and order, that comes after the primal image that you wish to maintain. That's my natural history. Because otherwise it's "Oystrygods gagging fishygods." But once you get a poem in there, once you get a poetic vision of what life could be, then people say, "This is what we want. If we're going to struggle for something, let's struggle in the interest of that."

RM: It strikes me, then, that what you're saying is that farce is always the appropriate response to the human condition, no matter what the time is.

AM: Yes. Americans get the idea that they only clash because of race and color, but that just leaves out the whole history of the world as we know it. Tribal warfare is also a matter of survival. Perhaps the matter of oystry- and fishygods is a confusion of aesthetic and moral orientation.

RM: You've talked about a number of writers who have been very important to you—Constance Rourke, Susanne Langer, Thomas Mann, to name just a few—but is there any writer who has caused you to change, as in making a 180 degree turn, in the way you've thought about something?

AM: I'm not aware of a 180 degree change, but there are books and writers who have helped me see other dimensions. There's *Horizon of Experience* by C. Delisle Burns. He was an English writer and professor. I read another book by him called *The First Europeans.* To really get to the bottom of what I talk about, you really have to go back into the history of Europe and the fall of Rome and into the Dark Ages and out. Then you see some things that add up to Homo Europaeus, which is Western man and of which Homo Americanus is the colonial, overseas cutting edge. In other words, we are the following of Homo Europaeus—Western man, Western human sensibility. To go back gives a sense of what horizon was, of what perception was at various points in history. It expands the problems that you face when you deal with provincialism. See, you can be provincial, that's because you're in the country, that's because you're isolated, but any time you get a point of view, a configuration, or a way of looking, that, generically speaking, is also about provincialism. So the least provincial people are the Europeans. That's why I say they invented the earth. The book that led me to that is up on the shelf: *The Worldwide Adventure of the Europeans,* by Denis de Rougement. It's about the beginning of Europe.

You've got Greek logic, Roman administration, and Judeo-Christian morality. But you can't get to Judeo-Christian unless you go through the Dark Ages and come out of that. The Romans were not Europeans. The Greeks were not Europeans. Europe evolved out of the Dark Ages. When we get into the Middle Ages, we have Europe and the Church. Then they discovered the Greek and Roman stuff, which added up to the period of the Renaissance, a European phenomenon—*The Worldwide Adventure of the Europeans.* Then the Europeans in effect invented the earth, which did not exist as a concept until they put it there. You realize that, don't you? The Japanese were where they lived, the Chinese were where they lived, and the Indians lived where they lived, and the Aztecs lived where they lived, Incas lived where they lived. But they didn't know where they were. [Chuckles.] Who knew? Magellan and those guys: "You're over here, you're over here, you're here. Now, this we call the Pacific Ocean. This is an ocean. Now this we call a continent. This whole thing is like a ball. Did you know that?" "No, anybody can see that this is flat." [Laughs.]

RM: When were you reading this?

AM: I discovered this when I was a young teacher. I started pulling this stuff together after I finished college. Then it all came into focus. A book like this developed my respect for what I'd guess I'd have to call the primacy of the all-purpose literary intellectual.

Here's a book, *Literary Opinion in America,* edited by Morton Dauwen Zabel, which was also important to me: "Essays illustrating the status, methods, and problems of criticism in the United States" since World War I. He wrote this in 1937. I was in college then, and his book was reviewed in the *Nation* and the *New Republic* and so we had it in the library at Tuskegee. This had Eliot's "Tradition and the Individual Talent," an important essay for me on how to use everything that had come before. And it connects with what Wynton and I are doing with Jazz at Lincoln Center. If you want to write a quatrain, Eliot says, it should be informed with the whole history of poetry. If you're going to play four bars, you should have all that in your bones. They say, "Well, he's a classicist, he's a traditionalist," which implies that you're against change. But what is tradition? That which continues!

Another key book, for me and my development as a literary artist and intellectual, was *Freud, Goethe, Wagner,* by Thomas Mann. The single essay that had the biggest impact was Mann's "Freud and the Future"—there I really began to see where ritual came in.

RM: What year was it that you began to read Mann?

AM: I didn't discover Mann until 1939. I had discovered anthropology in the tenth grade, after which I took as my task the challenge to explain primordial forms, the universality of art. I realized that that was the way to understand a people, a culture—you had to go to the primitive level. Then there was Ralph Ellison, who became one of my closest literary friends while he was working on his first novel, and we spent a lot of time talking about the nature and function of literature, and one time he told me that he and Stanley Edgar Hyman had gotten deeply into Kenneth Burke. Burke wasn't news to me. I had been reading him by that time in Zabel's book, for instance. But it was Ellison who suggested that I take a closer look at Burke's approach to fundamentals.

MM: How did your parents figure in in helping you decide what you should do with your life?

AM: Their conception of developing me was that I was the exiled prince— someone who was made for some higher purpose.

RM: So they recognized that early on.

AM: Everybody did. But we were poor, so you had to do it yourself. I had to do it myself. They didn't even take up a collection to send me to college. I had to figure that out—by way of scholarships to get there and then those plus working to stay there.

RM: So they could be supportive in terms of saying, "Yes, that's a wonderful thing to do," but they couldn't give you any material support.

AM: That's right. But there were the expectations.

RM: They put the expectations out, and you had to live up to them?

AM: Exactly. And with two years of college, you'd be way beyond anybody in that neighborhood, where just finishing high school was a big deal.

MM: Did they have a vision of you as a doctor or lawyer or something particular?

AM: No. That's the thing that is Scooter's special problem—nobody really says what he should do.

RM: He just knows he's supposed to do something well.

AM: They said, "You'll find out. You're a genius." [Laughs.] Like Miss Lexine Metcalf says, "You may have to travel far and wide to find out what it is you're supposed to do." The fairy tale, the epic, all of that, that's the way those things work.

Index